This book belongs to:

LEISURE ARTS, INC.
Little Rock, Arkansas

EDITORIAL STAFF

Vice President and Editor-in-Chief: Anne Van Wagner Childs. *Executive Director:* Sandra Graham Case. *Editorial Director:* Susan Frantz Wiles. *Publications Director:* Carla Bentley. *Creative Art Director:* Gloria Bearden. *Production Art Director:* Melinda Stout. PRODUCTION — *Managing Editor:* Susan White Sullivan. *Senior Editor:* Andrea Ahlen. *Project Coordinators:* Stephanie Gail Sharp and Jennifer S. Potts. DESIGN — *Design Director:* Patricia Wallenfang Sowers. EDITORIAL — *Managing Editor:* Linda L. Trimble. *Associate Editor:* Terri Leming Davidson. *Assistant Editors:* Tammi Williamson Bradley, Robyn Sheffield-Edwards, and Darla Burdette Kelsay. *Copy Editor:* Laura Lee Weland. ART — *Book/Magazine Art Director:* Diane M. Hugo. *Senior Production Artist:* Stephen L. Mooningham. *Production Artists:* Faith R. Lloyd and Dana M. Morris. *Photography Stylists:* Christina Tiano Myers, Karen Hall, and Sondra Daniel. PROMOTIONS — *Managing Editors:* Tena Kelley Vaughn and Marjorie Ann Lacy. *Associate Editors:* Steven M. Cooper, Marla Shivers, and Dixie L. Morris. *Designer:* Rhonda H. Hestir. *Art Directors:* Jeff Curtis and Linda Lovette Smart. *Production Artist:* Leslie Loring Krebs. *Publishing Systems Administrator:* Cindy Lumpkin. *Publishing Systems Assistant:* Susan M. Gray.

BUSINESS STAFF

Publisher: Bruce Akin. *Vice President, Finance:* Tom Siebenmorgen. *Vice President, Retail Sales:* Thomas L. Carlisle. *Retail Sales Director:* Richard Tignor. *Vice President, Retail Marketing:* Pam Stebbins. *Retail Marketing Director:* Margaret Sweetin. *Retail Customer Services Manager:* Carolyn Pruss. *General Merchandise Manager:* Russ Barnett. *Distribution Director:* Ed M. Strackbein. *Vice President, Marketing:* Guy A. Crossley. *Marketing Manager:* Byron L. Taylor. *Print Production Manager:* Laura Lockhart. *Print Production Coordinator:* Nancy Reddick Baker.

CREDITS

PHOTOGRAPHY: Ken West, Larry Pennington, and Karen Busick Shirey of Peerless Photography, Little Rock, Arkansas, and Jerry R. Davis of Jerry Davis Photography, Little Rock, Arkansas. COLOR SEPARATIONS: Magna IV Color Imaging of Little Rock, Arkansas. PHOTO LOCATIONS: The homes of Dr. and Mrs. Jerry Holton and Duncan and Nancy Porter.

Library of Congress Catalog Number 95-81883
International Standard Book Number 1-57486-010-0

It was the eve of Christmas, the snow lay deep and white,
I sat beside my window and looked into the night;
I heard the church-bells ringing, I saw the bright stars shine,
And childhood came again to me with all its dreams divine.

— F. E. WEATHERLY

INTRODUCTION

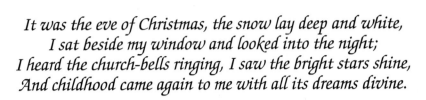

A treasury of nostalgic images, Once Upon a Christmastime pays tribute to the beautifully illustrated holiday storybooks so loved by the Victorians. Those delightfully naive tales, filled with the innocence and goodness of childhood, capture the true spirit of the holidays — and serve as a wonderful inspiration for our celebrations today! For this fanciful collection, we've assembled a splendid array of cross stitch designs inspired by vintage children's books. Woven together with those visions of holidays past are the colorful narratives of master storytellers, also borrowed from timeworn volumes. As you turn the pages, you'll rediscover the divine dreams of your childhood and find priceless gems to share with your family this season!

TABLE OF CONTENTS

TABLE OF CONTENTS

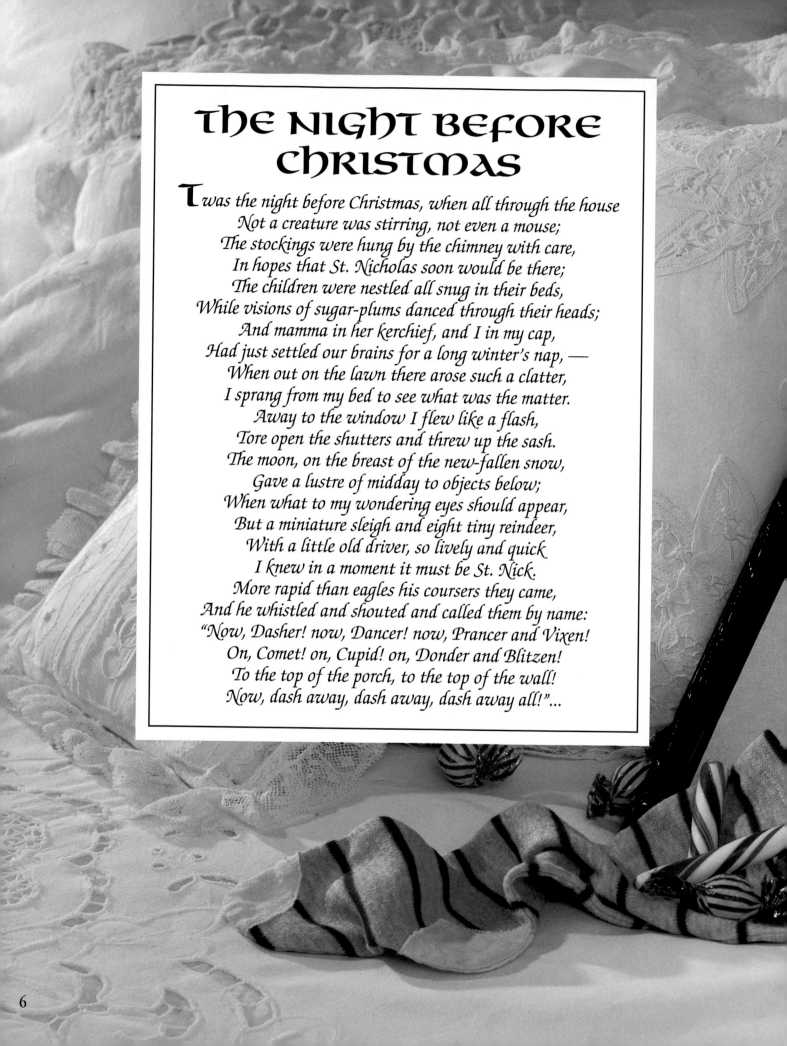

THE NIGHT BEFORE CHRISTMAS

Twas the night before Christmas, when all through the house
Not a creature was stirring, not even a mouse;
The stockings were hung by the chimney with care,
In hopes that St. Nicholas soon would be there;
The children were nestled all snug in their beds,
While visions of sugar-plums danced through their heads;
And mamma in her kerchief, and I in my cap,
Had just settled our brains for a long winter's nap, —
When out on the lawn there arose such a clatter,
I sprang from my bed to see what was the matter.
Away to the window I flew like a flash,
Tore open the shutters and threw up the sash.
The moon, on the breast of the new-fallen snow,
Gave a lustre of midday to objects below;
When what to my wondering eyes should appear,
But a miniature sleigh and eight tiny reindeer,
With a little old driver, so lively and quick
I knew in a moment it must be St. Nick.
More rapid than eagles his coursers they came,
And he whistled and shouted and called them by name:
"Now, Dasher! now, Dancer! now, Prancer and Vixen!
On, Comet! on, Cupid! on, Donder and Blitzen!
To the top of the porch, to the top of the wall!
Now, dash away, dash away, dash away all!"...

Chart on pages 52-53

As dry leaves that before the wild hurricane fly,
When they meet with an obstacle, mount to the sky,
So, up to the house-top the coursers they flew,
With the sleigh full of toys, — and St. Nicholas too.
And then in a twinkling I heard on the roof
The prancing and pawing of each little hoof.
As I drew in my head, and was turning around,
Down the chimney St. Nicholas came with a bound. ...

MERRY CHRISTMAS TO ALL
AND TO ALL A GOOD
NIGHT!

Chart on page 56

Chart on pages 50-51

He was dressed all in fur from his head to his foot,
And his clothes were all tarnished with ashes and soot;
A bundle of toys he had flung on his back,
And he looked like a peddler just opening his pack.
His eyes how they twinkled! his dimples how merry!
His cheeks were like roses, his nose like a cherry;
His droll little mouth was drawn up like a bow,
And the beard on his chin was as white as the snow.
The stump of a pipe he held tight in his teeth,
And the smoke it encircled his head like a wreath.
He had a broad face, and a little round belly
That shook, when he laughed, like a bowl full of jelly.
He was chubby and plump, — a right jolly old elf —
And I laughed when I saw him, in spite of myself.

Chart on page 56

A wink of his eye and a twist of his head
Soon gave me to know I had nothing to dread.
He spoke not a word, but went straight to his work,
And filled all the stockings; then turned with a jerk,
And laying his finger aside of his nose,
And giving a nod, up the chimney he rose. ...

Charts on page 57

Chart on pages 54-55

He sprang to his sleigh, to his team gave a whistle,
And away they all flew like the down of a thistle;
But I heard him exclaim, ere he drove out of sight:
"Happy Christmas to all, and to all a good-night!"

— CLEMENT CLARKE MOORE

Chart on page 57

13

FESTIVE SUGARPLUMS

Now don't complain — it's no use in the end,"
Said the big plum pudding to his Christmas friend,
"We've got to be eaten — that's why we're here —
We're part of the family Christmas cheer!
You don't hear me grumbling at my own lot —
Though the fire is fierce and the water is hot —
To be beautifully cooked and dished up in state —
Then eaten by the children — it's a lovely fate!"

Charts on pages 58 and 59

THE ANGELS' STORY

hark, and hear the old, old story
Angels tell each Christmas morn:
"Joy to Earth, to God the Glory;
Christ is come, and Love is born!"

Chart on pages 64-65

Chart on page 66

18

Glory to God

Peace on Earth

Love is Born

Rejoice

Christ is come

Charts on pages 63 and 67

19

PLAYING IN THE SNOW

But the best fun was when they tobogganing went,
That's a word by which, you must know, sleighing is meant.
They sat on their sleighs and they slid down the hill,
And now and then some of them had a fine spill.
If you'd heard how they laughed and had watched the fine fun,
You'd have said that of all sports, to sleigh was the one!

Charts on pages 68 and 69

WHO IS IT?

Now, children, there's somebody coming,
So try to think sharply and well;
And, when I get through with my story,
Just see if his name you can tell.

His hair is as white as a snow-drift;
But then he is not very old.
His coat is of fur at this season:
The weather, you know, is so cold.

He'll bring all the children a present,
The rich, and, I hope, too, the poor.
Some say that he comes down the chimney:
I think he comes in at the door.

His coat is all stuffed full of candy,
While all sorts of beautiful toys
You'll see sticking out of his pockets,
For girls just as well as for boys.

For girls he has dolls, muffs, and pictures;
For boys he has skates, or a sled:
And some little boys I can tell of,
Who will take horses with them to-bed.

And presents he brings for the mothers
And fathers and aunts with the rest;
But most he will bring for the children,
Because he likes little folks best.

I think you will know when you see him,
He's dressed up so funny and queer;
And then you'll hear every one shouting,
"MERRY CHRISTMAS
AND HAPPY NEW YEAR!"

Chart on pages 70-71

Chart on page 72

Chart on page 73

25

Noah's Ark

Is Santa Claus happy? There's no need to ask,
For he finds such enjoyment indeed in his task,
That he bubbles with laughter, and whistles and sings,
While making and planning the beautiful things.

There are gay Noah's Arks, just as full as can be
Of animals really a wonder to see;
There are lions, and tigers, and camels, and bears,
And two of each kind, for they travel in pairs.

There are elephants stretching their noses quite long;
And reindeer and elks with their antlers so strong,
And queer kangaroos all the others amid,
With their dear little babies in pockets well hid.

26

Charts on pages 60-62

27

GOOD CHILDREN ARE ST. NICK'S FAVORITES

St. Nick knows quite well who the good children are,
For wherever they may be he sees them afar.
On the top of his tower, with his spy-glass in hand,
He goes every morning to look o'er the land.

He peeps into houses whose doors are tight shut,
He looks through the mansion, and likewise the hut;
He gazes on cities and villages small,
And nothing, no, nothing is hidden at all.

He knows where the good children live beyond doubt,
He knows what the bad boys and girls are about,
And writes down their names on a page by themselves,
In books that he keeps on his library shelves.

For good girls and boys, truthful, gentle, and kind,
His prettiest presents and toys are designed;
While for those who are naughty, and love to do wrong,
He has a dislike that is hearty and strong.

So if you would please him, Dear Mary and Jack,
And win a nice prize from the old fellow's pack,
Be good little children, your parents obey,
And strive to be happy at work or at play.

Chart on page 75

ᕼe's a jolly good fellow, but ever so shy,
And likes to do all his good deeds on the sly,
So there's no use of spoiling a nice winter's nap,
For you'll not catch a glimpse of the jolly old chap.

When Christmas Eve comes, into bed you must creep,
And late in the night, when you all are asleep,
He is certain to come; so your stockings prepare,
And hang them up close by the chimney with care.

Chart on page 74

The baby's wee stocking
you must not forget,
For Santa will have something
nice for the pet,
And those who are thoughtful
for others will find
The good saint at Christmas time
has them in mind.

Chart on page 76

Chart on page 76

Good
John
Elizabeth
Laura

Bad
Keith
Robert
Vanessa

Susan
Daniel
Carla
Andrea
Gail
Steve

Charts on pages 77 and 78

*O*n *Santa Claus hurries, and works with a will,*
For many tall Christmas trees he has to fill,
And load them with treasures from out his rich store
Till they blossom as trees never blossomed before.

Chart on page 79

CHRISTMAS GUARDIAN

Love came down at Christmas,
Love all lovely, Love Divine;
Love was born at Christmas,
Star and angels gave the sign.

— CHRISTINA ROSSETTI

Chart on page 80

WOODLAND CHRISTMAS

Oh, Christmas is a jolly time
When forests hang with snow,
And other forests bend with toys,
And lordly Yule logs glow.

And Christmas is a solemn time
Because, beneath the star,
The first great Christmas Gift was given
To all men, near and far.

— FLORENCE EVELYN DRATT

Chart on page 83

I heard a bird sing
In the dark of December
A magical thing
And sweet to remember.

— OLIVER HERFORD

Chart on page 85

Chart on page 82

Out yonder in the moonlight, wherein God's acre lies,
Go angels walking to and fro, singing their lullabies.
Their radiant wings are folded, and their eyes are bended low,
As they sing among the beds whereon the flowers delight to grow.

— EUGENE FIELD

Charts on page 84

39

A FINE CHRISTMAS SNOW MAN

Outside all the meadows were covered with snow,
And soon a big snow man stood out there, you know,
With umbrella, and kerchief, and hat on his head,
"Here's a fine Christmas snow man!" the boys and girls said.

Chart on page 86

THE KIND OF LETTERS SANTA CLAUS LIKES

Attentively does Santa read the letters he receives,
And that he gets good hints from them he thoroughly believes;
For he looks below the surface, and can see between the lines,
Of goodness or of naughtiness the tell-tale marks and signs.

A grasping disposition he will readily detect;
And vainly those betraying selfish natures will expect
Nice presents to receive from him; such children he despises,
And gives them very frequently most painful, sad surprises.

So, one who writes a letter should most carefully avoid
A greedy spirit showing, for at that he'd be annoyed:
"This youngster seems to want the earth," in anger he might say,
And leave an empty stocking his resentment to display.

While one who, on the contrary, has sense and taste to write
A moderate petition, nicely worded and polite,
The high esteem of Santa Claus is sure thereby to gain,
And will not of his presents have occasion to complain.

The Night Before Christmas

MERRY

Chart on page 87

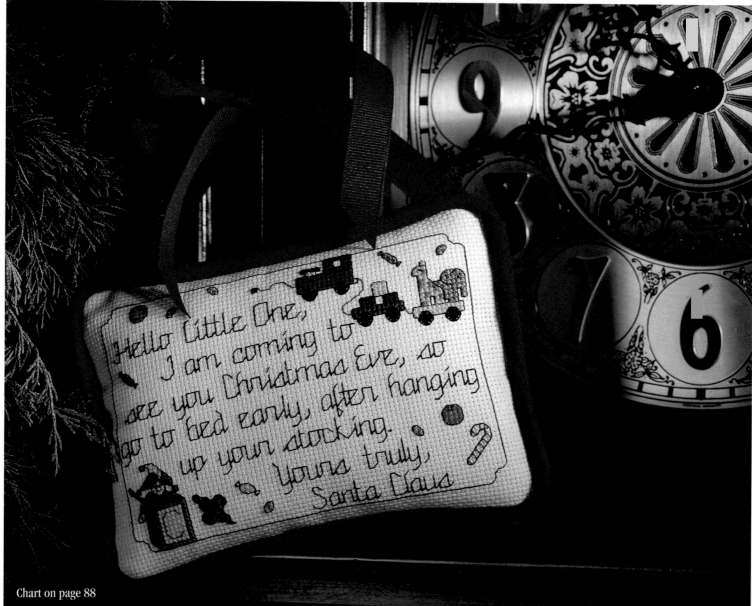

Chart on page 88

Dear Santa,
    Dolly and me
have both been
as good as good
can be. So don't
forget us on
Christmas day.
    affectionately,
Dolly and May

Dear Santa,
    I've been a
good boy this
year. If you
have some toys
left over, I sure
would like one.
    Your pal,
    Billy

SANTA CLAUS READING THE LETTERS.

Charts on pages 87 and 89

45

CHILDREN'S CHORUS

We bless his birth, who came to earth,
And in his cradle lowly
Received the earliest Christmas gifts, —
The Christ-child, pure and holy.
To him we raise our thanks and praise
For all the love he bore us;
For his dear sake our hymn we make,
And swell the Christmas chorus.

Chart on page 94

LONG MAY HE LIVE!

Then let us be glad, so that Christmas may be
A real Merry Christmas to you and to me:
And now that the story is ended we'll give
Three cheers for old Santa Claus! Long may he live!

Chart on pages 92-93

THE NIGHT BEFORE CHRISTMAS

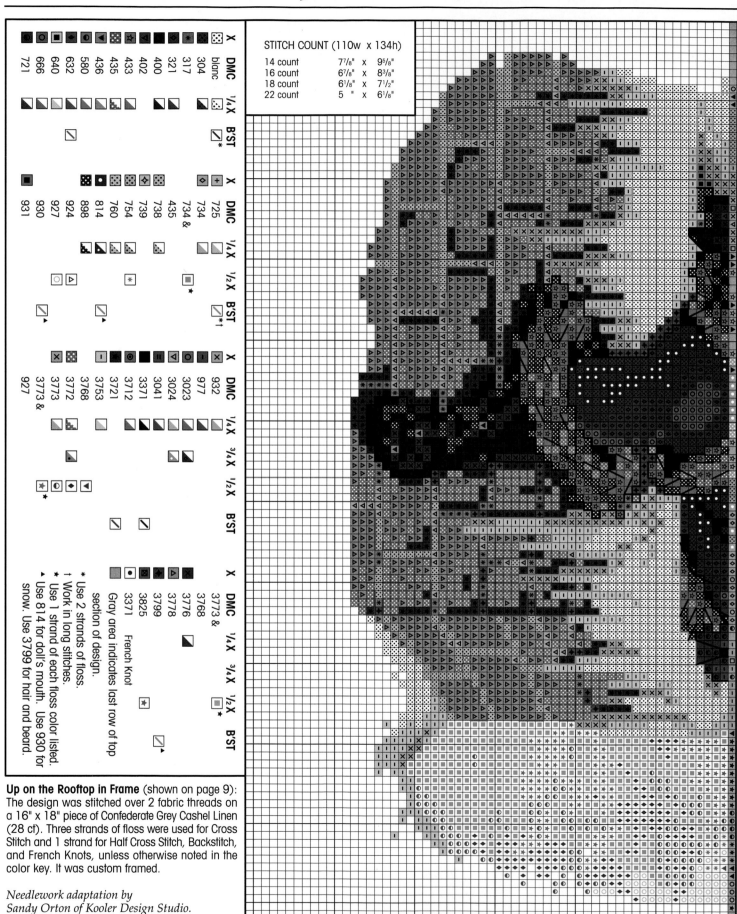

STITCH COUNT (110w x 134h)

14 count	7⁷⁄₈"	x 9⁵⁄₈"
16 count	6⁷⁄₈"	x 8³⁄₈"
18 count	6¹⁄₈"	x 7¹⁄₂"
22 count	5 "	x 6¹⁄₈"

Up on the Rooftop in Frame (shown on page 9): The design was stitched over 2 fabric threads on a 16" x 18" piece of Confederate Grey Cashel Linen (28 ct). Three strands of floss were used for Cross Stitch and 1 strand for Half Cross Stitch, Backstitch, and French Knots, unless otherwise noted in the color key. It was custom framed.

Needlework adaptation by
Sandy Orton of Kooler Design Studio.

50

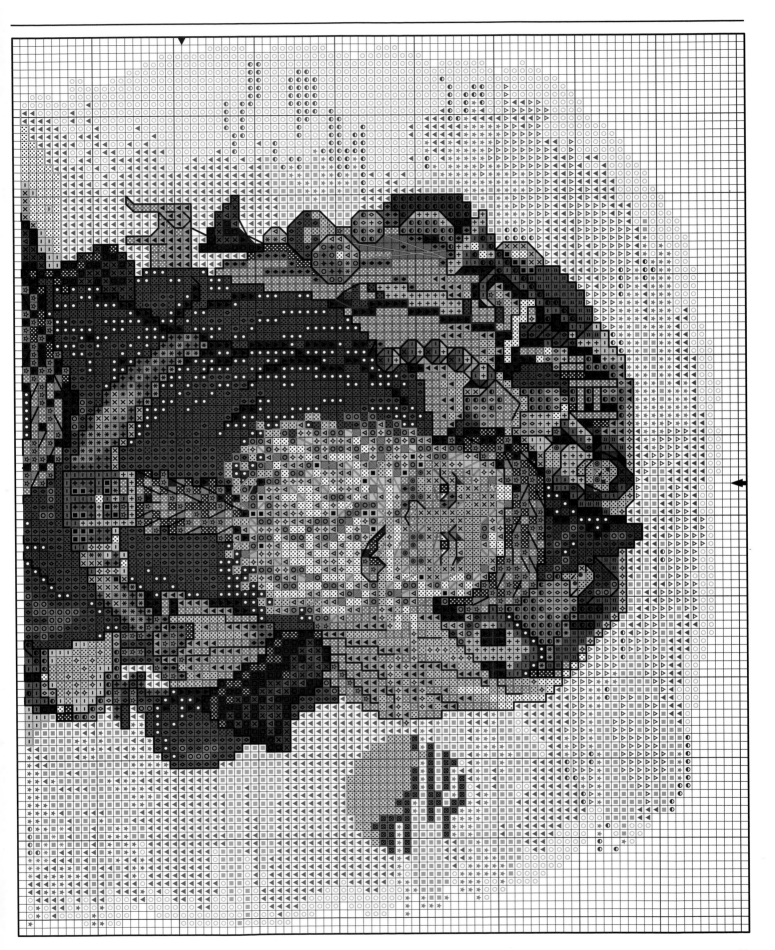

the NIGHT BEFORE christmas

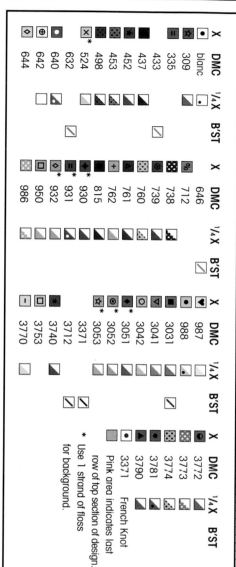

X							DMC	1/4X	B'ST
◇	⊕	▣	⊠	▨	▦	★	●		
			*						
							644		
							642		
							640	◪	
							632		◪
							524	▨	
							498	▨	
							453	▨	
							452	▨	
							437	◪	◪
							433		
							335		
							309		
							blanc		

X										DMC	1/4X	B'ST
▨	▢	◇	▮	▮	■	▨	+	▨	▨	646	▨	
			*	*	*					712	▨	
										738	▨	
										739	▨	
										760	▨	
										761	▨	◪
										762	◪	
										815	▨	
										930	▨	
										931	▨	
										932	◪	
										950		
										986		

X									DMC	1/4X	B'ST
▮	▢	✳	★	◉	◆	○	◁	■	●	▼	987
			*		*		*				988
											3031
											3041
											3042
											3051
											3052
											3053
											3371
											3712
											3740
											3753
											3770

X						DMC	1/4X	B'ST
▨	●	◐	●	◑	◉	3772	▨	
						3773	▨	◪
						3774	▨	
						3781	▨	
						3790	.	
						3371 French Knot	▨	◪

Pink area indicates last
row of top section of design.

* Use 1 strand of floss
for background.

Sleeping Children in Frame (shown on page 7): The design was stitched over 2 fabric threads on a 15" x 18" piece of Platinum Cashel Linen (28 ct). Three strands of floss were used for Cross Stitch and 1 strand for Backstitch and French Knot, unless otherwise noted in the color key. It was custom framed.

*Needlework adaptation by
Donna Vermillion Giampa.*

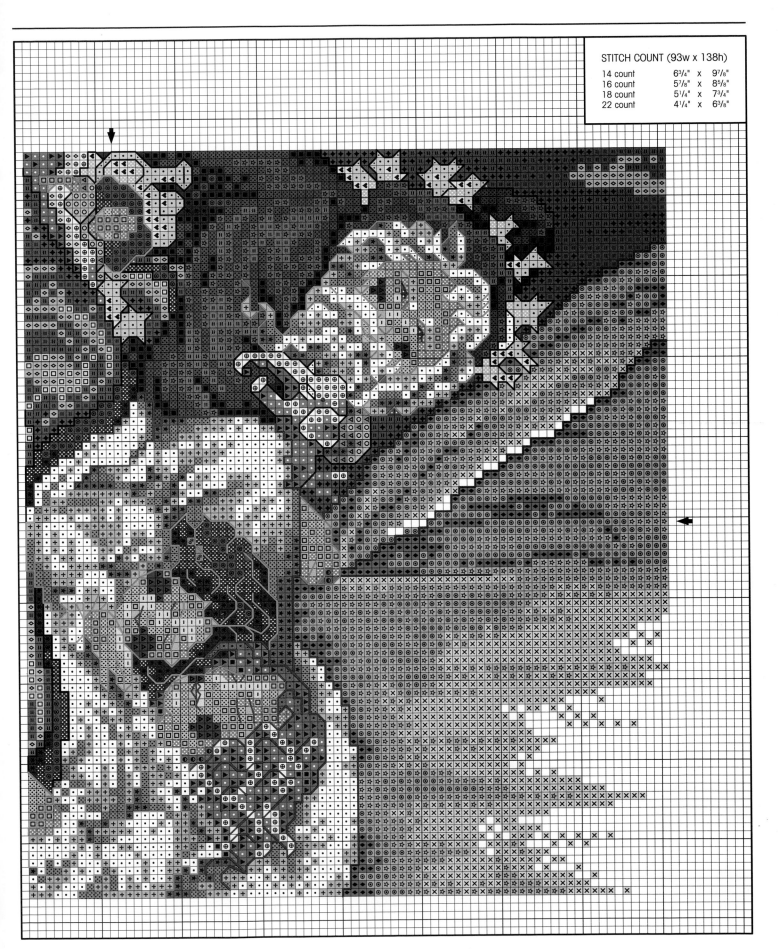

STITCH COUNT (93w x 138h)

14 count	6¾" x	9⅞"
16 count	5⅞" x	8⅝"
18 count	5¼" x	7¾"
22 count	4¼" x	6⅜"

THE NIGHT BEFORE CHRISTMAS

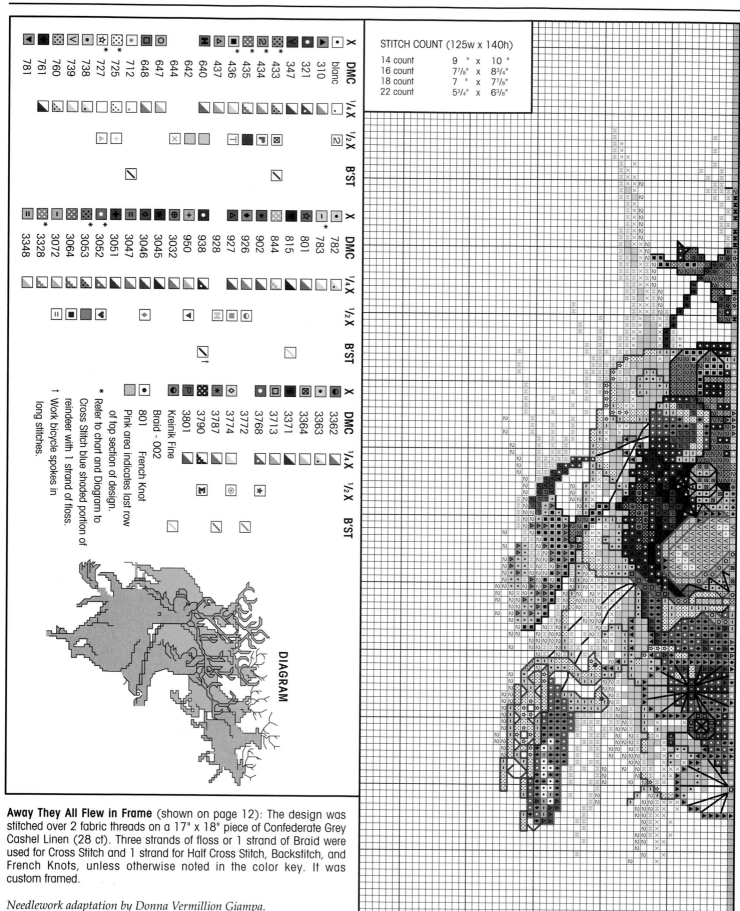

STITCH COUNT (125w x 140h)

count	width		height
14 count	9 "	x	10 "
16 count	7⅞"	x	8¾"
18 count	7 "	x	7⅞"
22 count	5¾"	x	6⅜"

DMC: 781, 761, 760, 739, 738, 727, 725, 712, 648, 647, 644, 642, 640, 437, 436, 435, 434, 433, 347, 321, 310, blanc

DMC: 3348, 3328, 3072, 3064, 3053, 3052, 3051, 3047, 3046, 3045, 3032, 950, 938, 928, 927, 926, 902, 844, 815, 801, 783, 782

DMC: 3801, 3790, 3787, 3774, 3772, 3768, 3713, 3371, 3364, 3363, 3362

801 — French Knot
Braid - 002
Kreinik Fine

* Refer to chart and Diagram to
Cross Stitch blue shaded portion of
of top section of design.

Pink area indicates last row
of top section of design.

† Work bicycle spokes in
long stitches.

Work reindeer with 1 strand of floss.

DIAGRAM

Away They All Flew in Frame (shown on page 12): The design was stitched over 2 fabric threads on a 17" x 18" piece of Confederate Grey Cashel Linen (28 ct). Three strands of floss or 1 strand of Braid were used for Cross Stitch and 1 strand for Half Cross Stitch, Backstitch, and French Knots, unless otherwise noted in the color key. It was custom framed.

Needlework adaptation by Donna Vermillion Giampa.

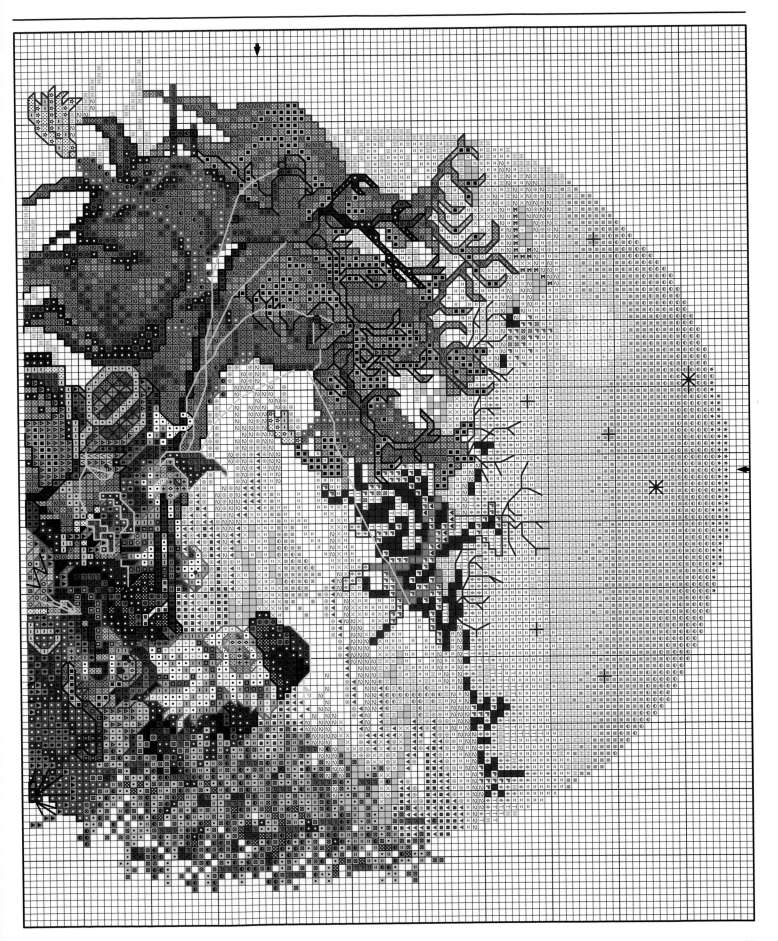

THE NIGHT BEFORE CHRISTMAS

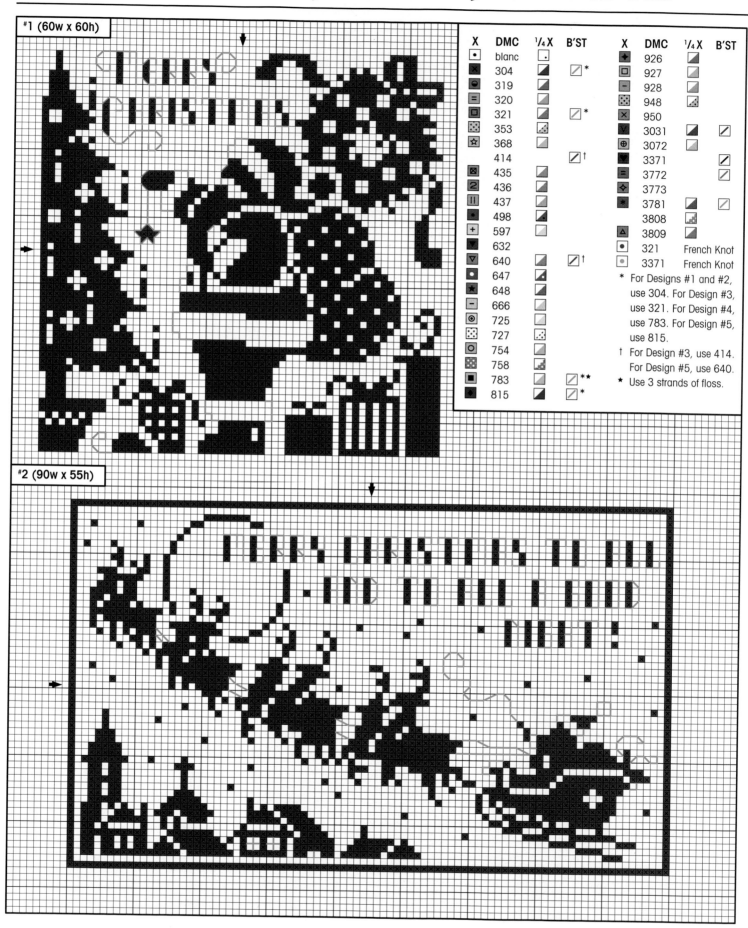

X	DMC	¼X	B'ST	X	DMC	¼X	B'ST
•	blanc	•		✦	926	◨	
✕	304	◪	◿ *	◻	927	◨	
◙	319	◨		–	928	◨	
◫	320	◨		⁚	948	◪	
▣	321	◨	◿ *	✕	950	◨	
▨	353	▨		▼	3031	◨	◿
★	368	◨		⊕	3072	◨	
	414		◿ †	◼	3371		◿
⊠	435	◨		▤	3772		◿
2	436	◨		✦	3773	◨	
‖	437	◨		✱	3781	◨	◿
⬤	498	◨			3808	◪	
+	597	◨		△	3809	◨	
▼	632			•	321		French Knot
▽	640	◨	◿ †	•	3371		French Knot
⬤	647	◪					
★	648	◨					
–	666	◨					
⊙	725	◨					
⁚	727	⁚					
○	754	◨					
⁚	758	◪					
▪	783	◨	◿ **				
✦	815	◨	◿ *				

* For Designs #1 and #2, use 304. For Design #3, use 321. For Design #4, use 783. For Design #5, use 815.

† For Design #3, use 414. For Design #5, use 640.

* Use 3 strands of floss.

#3 (36w x 50h)

#4 (36w x 49h)

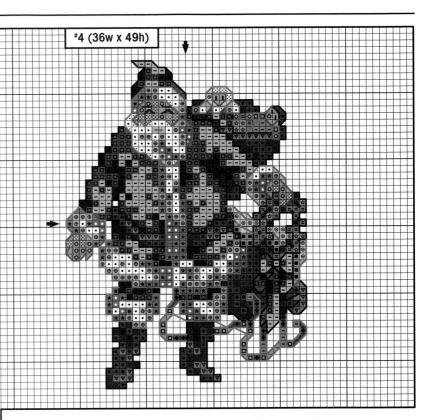

#5 (36w x 76h)

Straight to His Work Gift Bag (shown on page 10): Design #1 was stitched on a 16" x 27" piece of Hickory Heatherfield (8 ct). For placement, center design horizontally with bottom of design 5¹/₂" from one short edge of fabric. Six strands of floss were used for Cross Stitch and 2 strands for Backstitch. To complete bag, see Finishing Instructions, page 59.

"Merry Christmas to All" Pillow (shown on page 8): Design #2 was stitched on a 13" x 10" piece of Parchment Hearthstone (14 ct). Three strands of floss were used for Cross Stitch and 2 strands for Backstitch. For pillow, you will need a 9" x 6³/₄" piece of fabric for backing, 5¹/₂" x 56" fabric strip for ruffle (pieced as necessary), 2" x 29" bias fabric strip for cording, 29" length of ¹/₄" dia. purchased cord, and polyester fiberfill.
    Centering design, trim stitched piece to measure 9" x 6³/₄".
    To complete pillow, see Finishing Instructions, page 81.

Designs by Deborah Lambein.

The Night Before Christmas Stockings (shown on page 11): Designs #3 and #4 were each stitched on a 10" x 17" piece of Parchment Hearthstone (14 ct). For placement, center design horizontally with top of design 3" from one long edge of fabric. Three strands of floss were used for Cross Stitch and 1 strand for Backstitch and French Knots, unless otherwise noted in the color key. To complete stockings, see Finishing Instructions, page 96.

Needlework adaptations by Donna Vermillion Giampa.

"Merry Christmas to All" Ornament (shown on page 13): Design #5 was stitched over 2 fabric threads on a 7" x 11" piece of Confederate Grey Cashel Linen (28 ct). Three strands of floss were used for Cross Stitch and 1 strand for Backstitch.
    For ornament, you will need 3¹/₂" bellpull hardware.
    Centering design, trim stitched piece to measure 4¹/₂" x 8¹/₂". Measure ⁵/₈" from bottom of design and pull out one horizontal fabric thread. Fringe up to missing fabric thread. On each long edge turn fabric ¹/₄" to wrong side and press; turn ¹/₄" to wrong side again and hem. For casing at top edge, turn raw edge ¹/₄" to wrong side and press; turn ³/₄" to wrong side again and hem. Insert bellpull hardware.

Design by Linda Culp Calhoun.

FESTIVE SUGARPLUMS

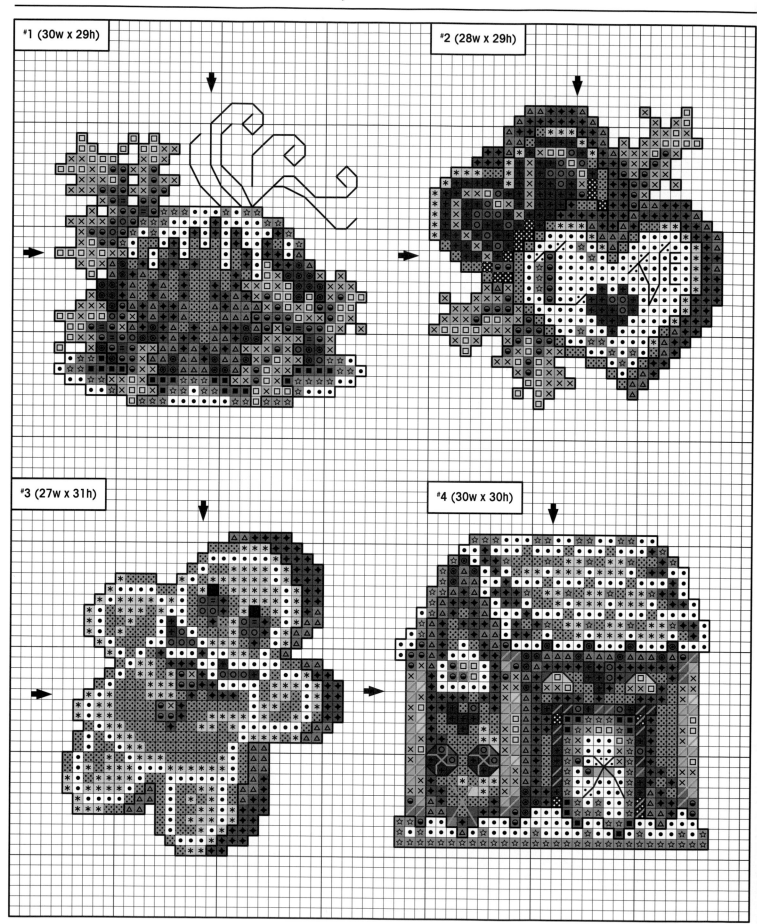

#1 (30w x 29h)

#2 (28w x 29h)

#3 (27w x 31h)

#4 (30w x 30h)

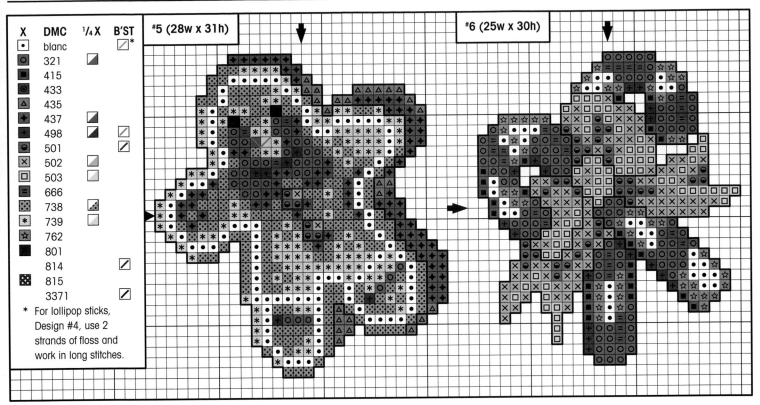

X	DMC	¼X	B'ST
·	blanc		◪*
◉	321	◪	
■	415		
◉	433		
△	435		
◆	437	◪	
✚	498	◪	◪
◉	501		◪
✕	502	◪	
▢	503	◪	
=	666		
▨	738	◪	
*	739	◪	
☆	762		
■	801		
	814		◪
▨	815		◪
	3371		◪

* For lollipop sticks, Design #4, use 2 strands of floss and work in long stitches.

#5 (28w x 31h) **#6 (25w x 30h)**

Sugarplum Ornaments (shown on page 15): Each design was stitched on a 4" square of Ecru perforated paper (14 ct), omitting quarter stitches in Design #4. Three strands of floss were used for Cross Stitch and 1 strand for Backstitch, unless otherwise noted in the color key. Referring to photo, trim perforated paper close to edges of each stitched design.

For each ornament, you will need a 4" square of fabric, 4" square of poster board, 4" square of paper-backed fusible web, rickrack, ⅛"w ribbon, buttons, and clear-drying craft glue.

Following manufacturer's directions for paper-backed fusible web, fuse fabric to poster board.

For round ornament, trim fabric-covered poster board to a 3½" dia. circle. Center stitched piece on ornament front and glue in place; glue an 11¼" length of rickrack around edge of ornament front. For hanger, fold 4" length of ribbon in half and glue ends at top center of ornament front. Tie 6" length of ribbon in a bow and, referring to photo, glue to top center of ornament front, covering ends of hanger. Glue button at center of bow.

For square ornament, trim fabric-covered poster board to a 3½" square. Center stitched piece on ornament front and glue in place. Referring to photo for placement, glue a 3½" length of rickrack across top and bottom of ornament; for hanger, glue a 7½" length of ribbon and buttons to ornament.

Plum Pudding Gift Tag (shown on page 14): Design #1 was stitched on a 4" square of Ecru perforated paper (14 ct). Three strands of floss were used for Cross Stitch and 1 strand for Backstitch.

For gift tag, you will need a 7" x 4" piece of fabric, 7" x 4" piece of heavy brown paper, 7" x 4" piece of paper-backed fusible web, 4 buttons, 23" length of ⅛"w ribbon for hanger, and clear-drying craft glue.

Centering design, trim stitched piece to a 2½" square.

Following manufacturer's directions for paper-backed fusible web, fuse fabric to paper. Trim fabric-covered paper to a 6⅜" x 3⅛" rectangle; matching short edges, fold paper in half. Center stitched piece on front of gift tag and glue in place. Referring to photo, glue button at each corner of stitched piece. Referring to photo, use a sharp object to make a hole through both layers of gift tag close to button at top left corner. Fold ribbon in half and insert both ends of ribbon from back of gift tag through both holes; thread ends of ribbon through loop and pull to secure.

Hearts Mug (shown on page 14): Design #2 was stitched on a 10¼" x 3½" Parchment Vinyl-Weave™ (14 ct) mug insert. Three strands of floss were used for Cross Stitch and 1 strand for Backstitch. It was inserted in a Parchment Mugs-Your-Way™ Mug.

For design placement, fold Vinyl-Weave™ in half, matching short edges. Center design on right half of vinyl if mug is to be used by a right-handed person and on left half of vinyl if mug is to be used by a left-handed person. Hand wash mug to protect stitchery.

Gingerbread Towels (shown on page 14): Designs #3 and #5 were stitched on the Aida (14 ct) border of a Vanilla/Cranberry Check Kitchen Classic towel, aligning the bottom of the designs and leaving 8 spaces between designs. Design #4 was stitched on the Aida (14 ct) border of a Vanilla/Evergreen Check Kitchen Classic towel. Three strands of floss were used for Cross Stitch and 1 strand for Backstitch, unless otherwise noted in the color key.

Candy Cane Bread Cloth (shown on page 15): Design #6 was stitched on one corner of an Ivory Royal Classic Breadcover (14 ct) with design 7 fabric threads from beginning of fringe. Three strands of floss were used for Cross Stitch and 1 strand for Backstitch.

Designs by Donna Vermillion Giampa.

FINISHING INSTRUCTIONS

Straight to His Work Gift Bag (shown on page 10, chart on page 56): For bag, you will need a 16" x 27" piece of Hickory Heatherfield for backing and 54" length of ¼" dia. satin cording.

Matching right sides and leaving top edge open, use a ½" seam allowance to sew stitched piece and backing fabric together. Trim seam allowances diagonally at corners and press seam allowances open. To form bottom corners, place right sides together, matching side seams to bottom seam. Sew diagonally across each corner 1" from point of corner.

Turn top edge of bag ½" to wrong side and press; turn ¾" to wrong side again and hem. Turn bag right side out. Tie an overhand knot at ends of cording and tie cording around top of bag as desired.

NOAh's ARk

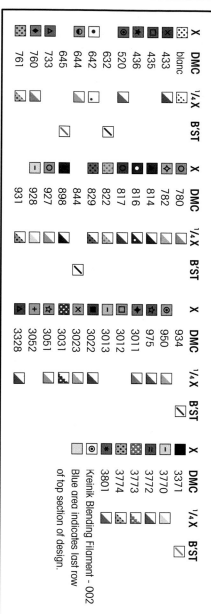

X												DMC	1/4 X	B'ST
												761		
												760		
												733		
												645		
												644		
												642		
												632		
												520		
												436		
												435		
												433		
												blanc		

DMC — 780, 782, 814, 816, 817, 822, 829, 844, 898, 927, 928, 931

DMC — 934, 950, 975, 3011, 3012, 3013, 3022, 3023, 3031, 3051, 3052, 3328

DMC — 3371, 3770, 3772, 3773, 3774, 3801

Kreinik Blending Filament - 002

Blue area indicates last row of top section of design.

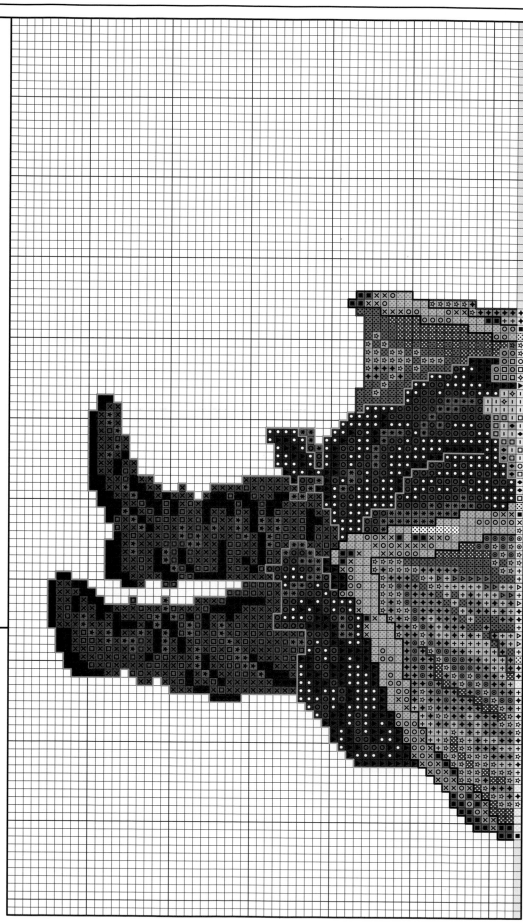

Noah's Ark in Frame (shown on page 27): The design was stitched over 2 fabric threads on a 15" x 17" piece of Summer Khaki Belfast Linen (32 ct). Two strands of floss or Blending Filament were used for Cross Stitch and 1 strand for Backstitch. It was custom framed.

Needlework adaptation by Donna Vermillion Giampa.

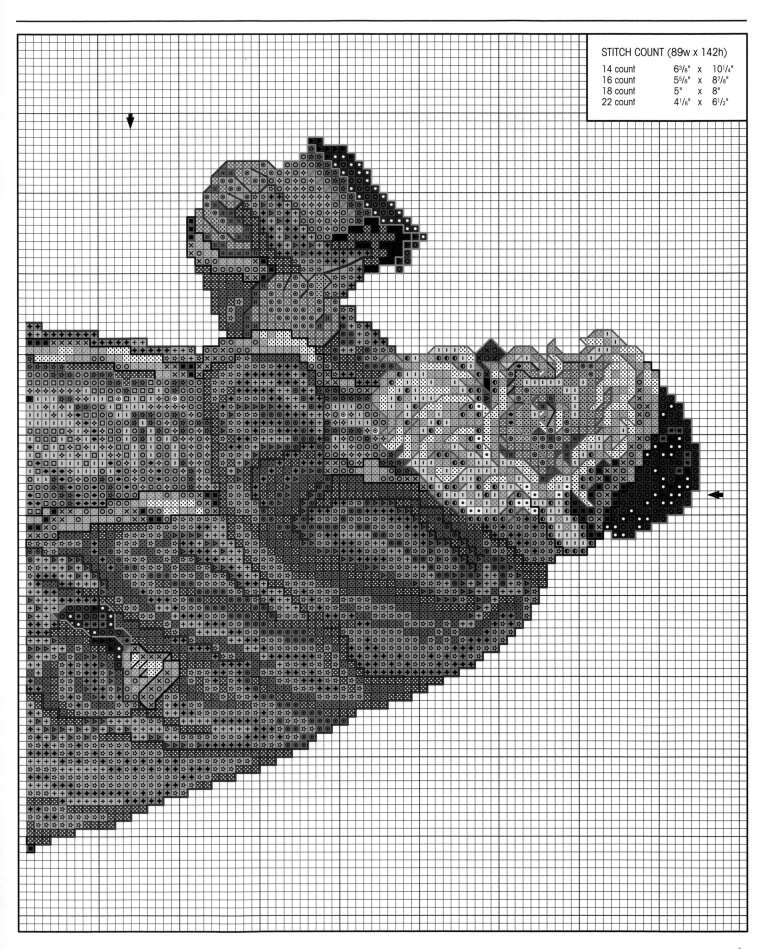

STITCH COUNT (89w x 142h)

14 count	6³/₈" x	10¹/₄"
16 count	5⁵/₈" x	8⁷/₈"
18 count	5" x	8"
22 count	4¹/₈" x	6¹/₂"

Noah's ark

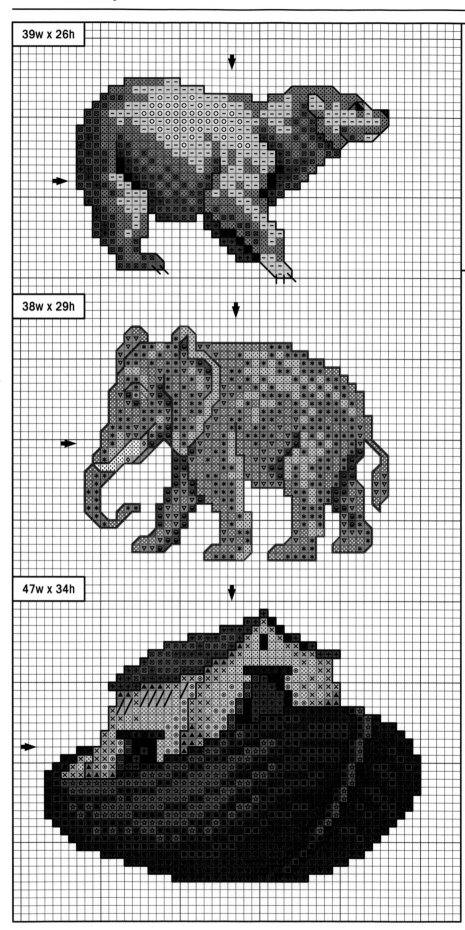

39w x 26h

38w x 29h

47w x 34h

X	DMC	¼ X	B'ST	X	DMC	¼ X	B'ST
⊡	blanc	⊡			844		◪
▨	310		◪	■	898	◪	
✦	433			▽*	926 &		◪
⊠	435	◪			3022		
⊠	436	◪		⊙	928		
▲	642			⊠	3022	◪	
✕	644			✳	3023	◪	
◕	645	◪		◇	3024	◪	
–	738	◪			3371		◪
○	739			✪	3801		
◼	814			⊙	blanc	French Knot	
▣	816						
▪	817			* Use 1 strand of each			
⊡	822	◪		floss color listed.			

Noah's Ark Ornaments (shown on pages 26-27): Each design was stitched over 2 fabric threads on a 7" x 6" piece of Summer Khaki Belfast Linen (32 ct). Two strands of floss were used for Cross Stitch, 1 strand for Backstitch and French Knot, and 4 strands for Blanket Stitch.

For each ornament, you will need a 7" x 6" piece of Summer Khaki Belfast Linen for backing, tracing paper, fabric marking pencil, polyester fiberfill, DMC 640 embroidery floss for Blanket Stitch, and 7" length of #20 jute twine.

For pattern, fold tracing paper in half and place fold on dashed line of desired pattern; trace pattern onto tracing paper. Cut out pattern; unfold and press flat. Centering pattern on wrong side of stitched piece, pin pattern in place. Use fabric marking pencil to draw around pattern; remove pattern. Matching right sides and raw edges, pin stitched piece and backing fabric together.

Leaving an opening for turning, use a short stitch length and sew directly on drawn line; remove pins. Trim seam allowance to ¼"; clip curves and turn ornament right side out. Lightly stuff ornament with polyester fiberfill and blind stitch opening closed.

Referring to photo and Blanket Stitch Instructions below, Blanket Stitch around ornament.

For hanger, fold jute in half; referring to photo for placement, tack ends of jute to ornament back.

BLANKET STITCH

Knot one end of floss. Bring needle up from wrong side at 1, even with edge of fabric. Go down at 2 and come up at 3, keeping floss below point of needle (**Fig. 1**). Continue to stitch in this manner, keeping tension even and stitches evenly spaced (**Fig. 2**).

Fig. 1

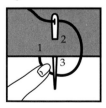

Fig. 2

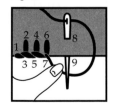

Designs by Donna Vermillion Giampa.

THE ANGELS' STORY

X	DMC	B'ST		X	DMC	B'ST
■	311	▨		=	676	
▣	347			☆	729	▨
◉	561			■	815	
▽	562			◉	3781	▨

Angels' Story Ornaments (shown on page 19): Each design was stitched on an 8" square of Antique White Belfast Linen (32 ct). Two strands of floss were used for Cross Stitch and 1 strand for Backstitch.

For each ornament, you will need an 8" square of Antique White Belfast Linen for backing, 7" x 4" piece of adhesive mounting board, tracing paper, pencil, 7" x 4" piece of batting, 12" length of ¼" dia. purchased cording with attached seam allowance, and clear-drying craft glue.

To complete ornaments, see Angels' Story Ornament Finishing, page 69.

Designs by Linda Culp Calhoun.

THE ANGELS' STORY

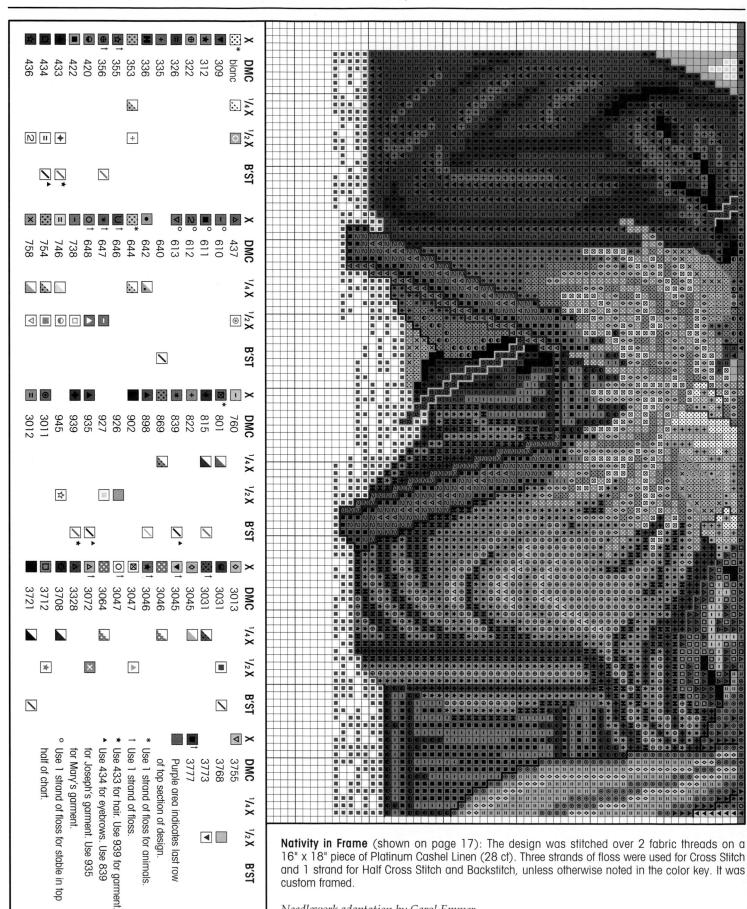

Color Key — DMC

X	1/4X	1/2X	B'ST	DMC
				blanc
				309
				312
				322
				326
				335
				336
				353
				355
				356
				420
				422
				433
				434
				436
				437
				610
				611
				612
				613
				640
				642
				644
				646
				647
				648
				738
				746
				754
				758
				760
				801
				815
				822
				839
				869
				898
				902
				926
				927
				935
				939
				945
				3011
				3012
				3013
				3031
				3045
				3046
				3047
				3064
				3072
				3328
				3708
				3712
				3721
				3755
				3768
				3773
				3777

* Purple area indicates last row of top section of design.
* Use 1 strand of floss for animals.
† Use 1 strand of floss.
★ Use 433 for hair. Use 939 for garment.
▶ Use 434 for eyebrows. Use 839 for Joseph's garment. Use 935 for Mary's garment.
° Use 1 strand of floss for stable in top half of chart.

Nativity in Frame (shown on page 17): The design was stitched over 2 fabric threads on a 16" x 18" piece of Platinum Cashel Linen (28 ct). Three strands of floss were used for Cross Stitch and 1 strand for Half Cross Stitch and Backstitch, unless otherwise noted in the color key. It was custom framed.

Needlework adaptation by Carol Emmer.

STITCH COUNT (104w x 145h)

14 count	7½"	x	10⅜"
16 count	6½"	x	9⅛"
18 count	5⅞"	x	8⅛"
22 count	4¾"	x	6⅝"

66w x 98h

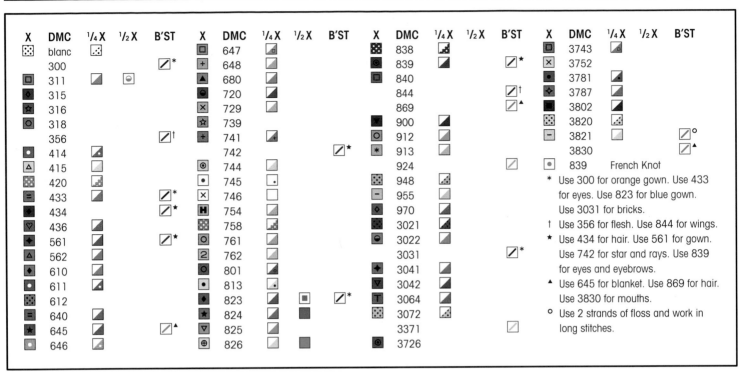

X	DMC	1/4X	1/2X	B'ST	X	DMC	1/4X	1/2X	B'ST	X	DMC	1/4X	1/2X	B'ST	X	DMC	1/4X	1/2X	B'ST
	blanc					647					838					3743			
	300			*		648					839			*		3752			
	311					680					840					3781			
	315					720					844			†		3787			
	316					729					869			▲		3802			
	318					739					900					3820			
	356			†		741					912					3821			°
	414					742			*		913					3830			▲
	415					744					924					839	French Knot		
	420					745					948								
	433			*		746					955								
	434			*		754					970								
	436					758					3021								
	561			*		761					3022								
	562					762					3031			*					
	610					801					3041								
	611					813					3042								
	612					823			*		3064								
	640					824					3072								
	645			▲		825					3371								
	646					826					3726								

* Use 300 for orange gown. Use 433 for eyes. Use 823 for blue gown. Use 3031 for bricks.

† Use 356 for flesh. Use 844 for wings.

★ Use 434 for hair. Use 561 for gown. Use 742 for star and rays. Use 839 for eyes and eyebrows.

▲ Use 645 for blanket. Use 869 for hair. Use 3830 for mouths.

° Use 2 strands of floss and work in long stitches.

36w x 53h

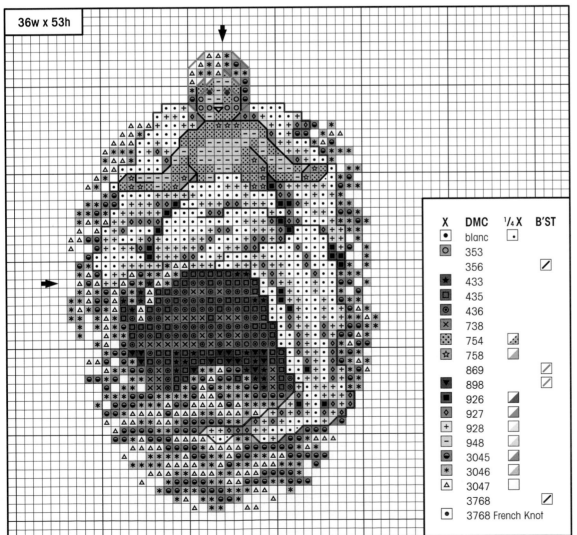

X	DMC	1/4X	B'ST
	blanc		
	353		
	356		
	433		
	435		
	436		
	738		
	754		
	758		
	869		
	898		
	926		
	927		
	928		
	948		
	3045		
	3046		
	3047		
	3768		
	3768 French Knot		

Angelic Attendants in Frame (shown on page 18): The design was stitched over 2 fabric threads on a 14" x 16" piece of Antique White Lugana (25 ct). Three strands of floss were used for Cross Stitch and 1 strand for Half Cross Stitch, Backstitch, and French Knots, unless otherwise noted in the color key. It was custom framed.

Needlework adaptation by Nancy Dockter.

Holy Infant in Frame (shown on page 19): The design was stitched over 2 fabric threads on a 9" square of Antique White Belfast Linen (32 ct). Two strands of floss were used for Cross Stitch and 1 strand for Backstitch and French Knots. It was inserted in an oval gold frame (3" x 4" opening).

Needlework adaptation by Donna Vermillion Giampa.

playing in the snow

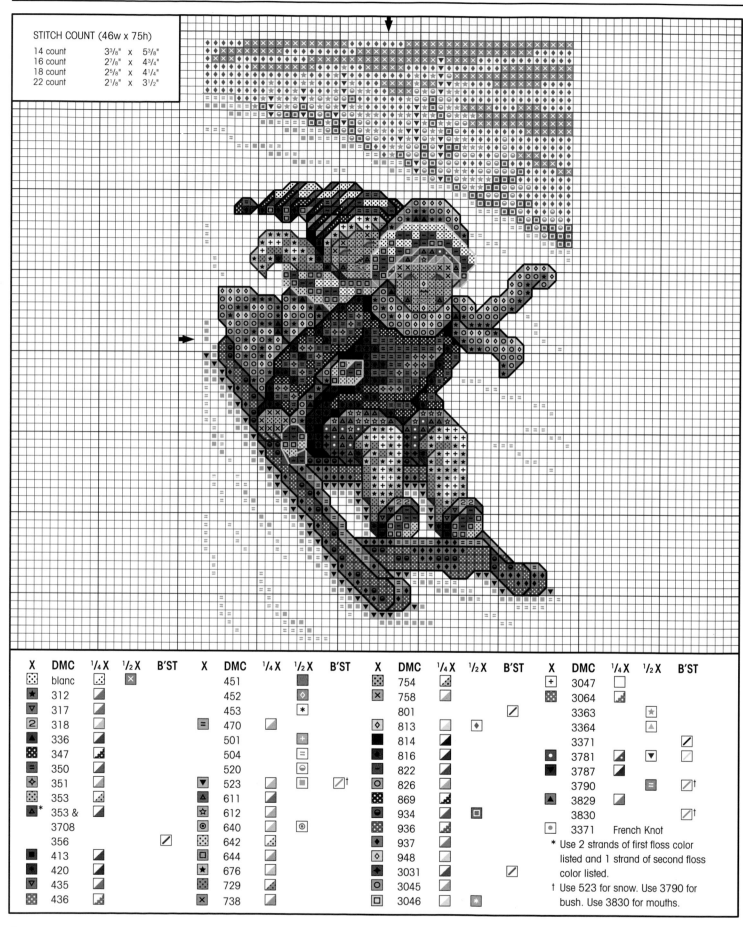

STITCH COUNT (46w x 75h)

14 count	3³/₈"	x	5³/₈"
16 count	2⁷/₈"	x	4³/₄"
18 count	2⁵/₈"	x	4¹/₄"
22 count	2¹/₈"	x	3¹/₂"

X	DMC	¼X	½X	B'ST	X	DMC	¼X	½X	B'ST	X	DMC	¼X	½X	B'ST	X	DMC	¼X	½X	B'ST
	blanc		X			451					754				+	3047			
★	312					452		◇		X	758					3064			
▽	317					453		*			801					3363		★	
2	318			=	470				◇	813		◆			3364		▲	
▲	336					501		+			814					3371			
	347					504		=			816					3781		▼	
=	350					520		⊖			822				▼	3787			
◆	351			▼	523		■	⁄†	○	826					3790		=	⁄†
	353			▲	611					869				▲	3829			
▲*	353 &			☆	612				●	934		▣			3830			⁄†
	3708			◉	640		◉			936				●	3371	French Knot
	356		⁄		642				◆	937								
■	413			□	644				◇	948			* Use 2 strands of first floss color
*	420			★	676					3031			⁄	listed and 1 strand of second floss
▼	435				729				○	3045			color listed.
	436			X	738				□	3046		*	† Use 523 for snow. Use 3790 for
															bush. Use 3830 for mouths.

68

FINISHING INSTRUCTIONS

Angels' Story Ornament Finishing (shown on page 19, charts and supplies on page 63): For pattern, fold tracing paper in half and place fold on dashed line of pattern; trace pattern onto tracing paper. Cut out pattern; unfold and press flat. Draw around pattern twice on mounting board and twice on batting; cut out. Remove paper from one piece of mounting board and press one batting piece onto mounting board. Repeat with remaining mounting board and batting.

Referring to photo, position pattern on wrong side of stitched piece; pin pattern in place. Cut stitched piece **1" larger** than pattern on all sides. Cut backing fabric same size as stitched piece. Clip ¹⁄₂" into edge of stitched piece at ¹⁄₂" intervals. Center wrong side of stitched piece over batting on one mounting board piece; fold edges of stitched piece to back of mounting board and glue in place. For ornament back, repeat with backing fabric and remaining mounting board.

Beginning and ending at top center of stitched piece, glue cording seam allowance to wrong side of ornament front, overlapping ends of cording. Matching wrong sides, glue ornament front and back together.

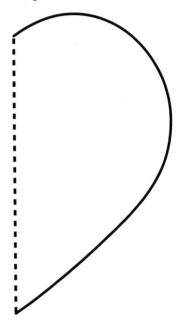

Playing in the Snow in Frames (shown on pages 20-21): Each design was stitched over 2 fabric threads on a 12" x 14" piece of Antique White Lugana (25 ct). Three strands of floss were used for Cross Stitch and 1 strand for Half Cross Stitch, Backstitch, and French Knots. They were custom framed.

Needlework adaptations by Nancy Dockter.

who is it?

Needlework adaptation by Donna Vermillion Giampa.

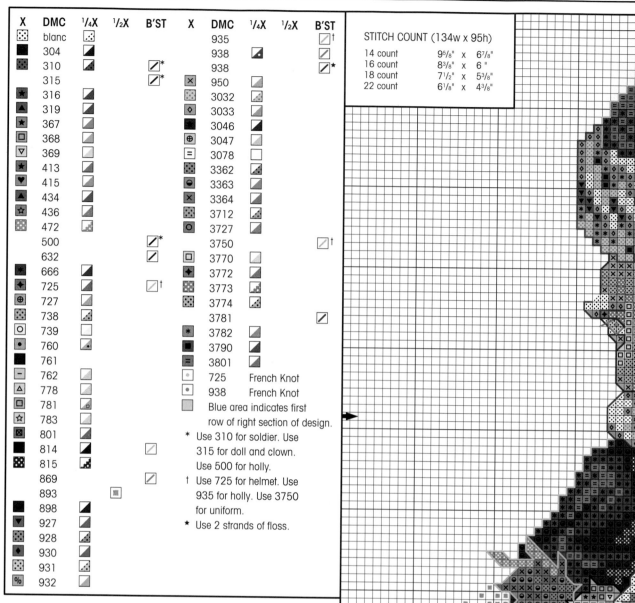

X	DMC	¼X	½X	B'ST	X	DMC	¼X	½X	B'ST
	blanc					935			/ †
	304	/				938	/		/
	310	/		/ *		938			/ *
	315			/ *		950		/	
	316	/				3032			
	319	/				3033	/		
	367	/				3046	/		
	368	/				3047	/		
	369	/				3078			
	413	/				3362	/		
	415	/				3363			
	434	/				3364			
	436	/				3712	/		
	472	/				3727			
	500			/ *		3750			/ †
	632	/				3770			
	666	/				3772	/		
	725	/		/ †		3773	/		
	727					3774	/		
	738	/				3781			/
	739					3782			
	760	/				3790	/		
	761					3801	/		
	762	/				725			French Knot
	778	/				938			French Knot
	781	/							
	783	/							
	801	/							
	814	/		/					
	815	/							
	869			/					
	893								
	898	/							
	927	/							
	928	/							
	930	/							
	931	/							
	932	/							

STITCH COUNT (134w x 95h)

14 count	9⅝"	x	6⅞"
16 count	8⅜"	x	6 "
18 count	7½"	x	5⅜"
22 count	6⅛"	x	4⅜"

Blue area indicates first row of right section of design.

* Use 310 for soldier. Use 315 for doll and clown. Use 500 for holly.

† Use 725 for helmet. Use 935 for holly. Use 3750 for uniform.

★ Use 2 strands of floss.

Who Is It in Frame (shown on page 23): The design was stitched over 2 fabric threads on a 19" x 16" piece of Ivory Lugana (25 ct). Three strands of floss were used for Cross Stitch, 1 strand for Half Cross Stitch and Backstitch, and 2 strands for French Knots, unless otherwise noted in the color key. It was custom framed.

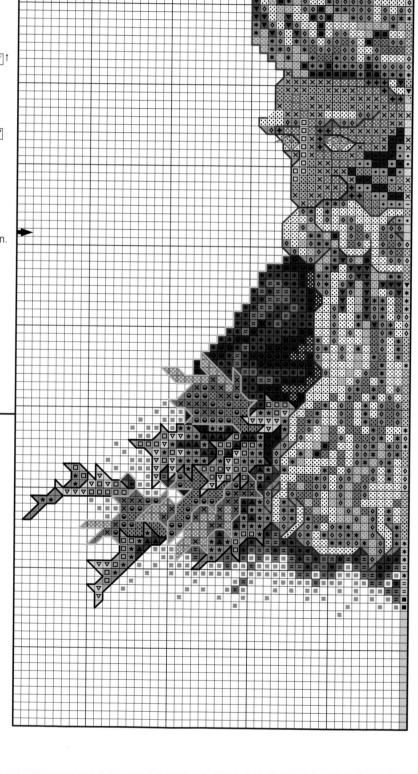

who is it?

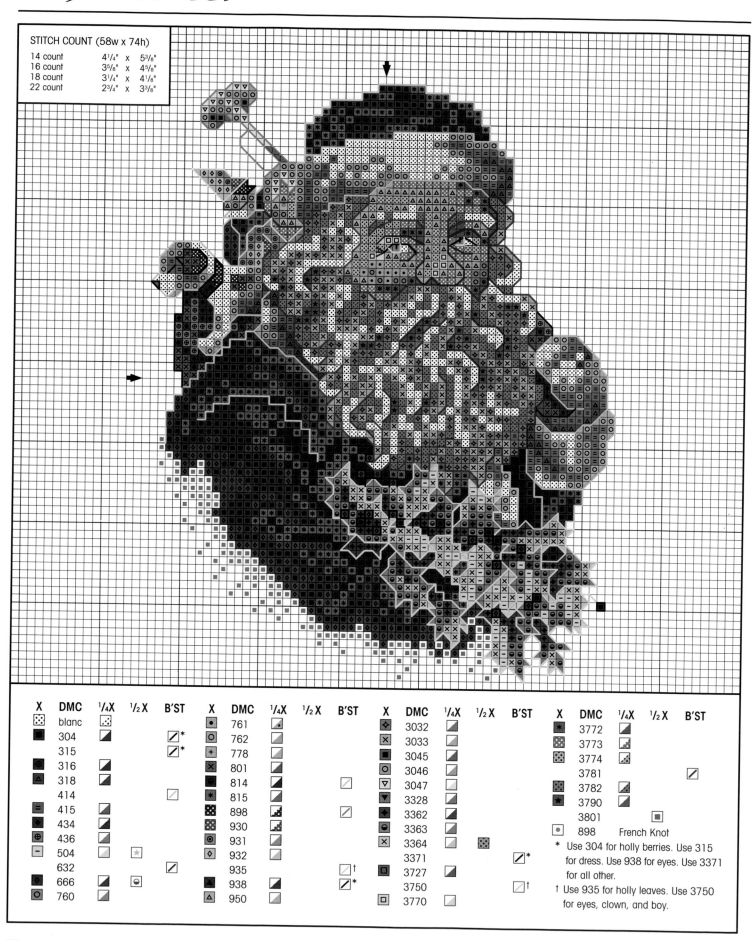

STITCH COUNT (51w x 79h)

14 count	3¾"	x 5¾"
16 count	3¼"	x 5"
18 count	2⅞"	x 4½"
22 count	2⅜"	x 3⅝"

Toys for Good Girls and Boys in Frames (shown on pages 24-25): Each design was stitched over 2 fabric threads on a 13" x 14" piece of Ivory Lugana (25 ct). Three strands of floss were used for Cross Stitch and 1 strand for Half Cross Stitch, Backstitch, and French Knots. They were custom framed.

Needlework adaptations by Donna Vermillion Giampa.

good children

X	DMC	1/4 X	B'ST
⊡	blanc	⊡	
	310		╱
▢	317		
	356		╱
✳	413	◪	
▨	414	▨	╱
◼	420	◪	
▲	422		
▨	451	◪	
◆	452	◪	
◼	535	◪	
▨	644	◪	
	645		╱
▢	676	◪	
⊞	677	◪	
◆	680	◪	
▨	729	▨	
★	743	◪	
○	745		
◇	754	◪	
◼	758	◪	
▨*	758 &	◪	
	3779		
☆	761		
▨	822	▨	
◼	840	◪	
▨	869		╱
–	927	◪	
◼	945		
▨	948	▨	
▢	950	◪	
✳	951		
▨	3021	▨	╱
☆	3023	◪	
▽	3024	◪	
▼	3041		
☆	3042		
⊟	3064	◪	
⊠	3326		
	3721		╱
◼	3740		
◼*	3740 &		
	3787		
◼	3772	◪	
▨*	3773 &	◪	
	452		
⊟	3779	◪	
⊙	3787	◪	
◼	3790	◪	
◆	3799	◪	
⊞	3828		

* Use 1 strand of each floss color listed.

STITCH COUNT (57w x 90h)

14 count	4¹/₈"	x	6¹/₂"
16 count	3⁵/₈"	x	5⁵/₈"
18 count	3¹/₄"	x	5"
22 count	2⁵/₈"	x	4¹/₈"

Waiting for St. Nick in Frame (shown on page 30): The design was stitched over 2 fabric threads on a 12" x 14" piece of Cream Belfast Linen (32 ct). Two strands of floss were used for Cross Stitch and 1 strand for Backstitch. It was custom framed.

Needlework adaptation by Nancy Dockter.

St. Nick with Book in Frame (shown on page 29): The design was stitched over 2 fabric threads on a 12" x 16" piece of Platinum Cashel Linen (28 ct). Three strands of floss were used for Cross Stitch and 1 strand for Half Cross Stitch, Backstitch, and French Knots. It was custom framed.

Needlework adaptation by Donna Vermillion Giampa.

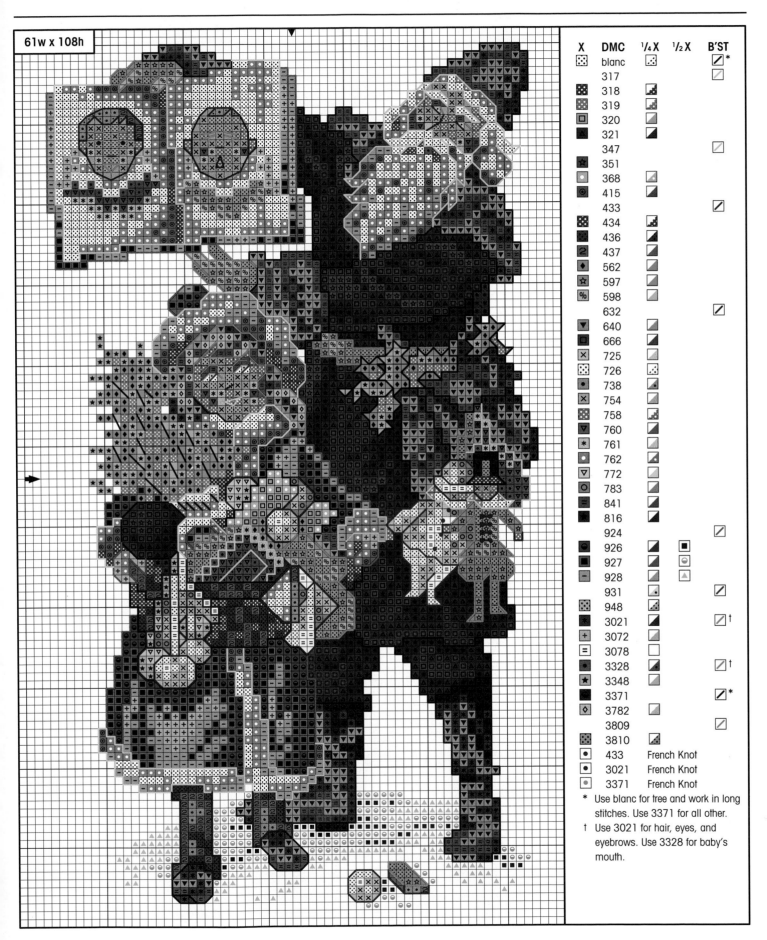

61w x 108h

X	DMC	¼X	½X	B'ST
⊡	blanc	⊡		⧄ *
	317			⧄
⊠	318	◪		
⊡	319	◪		
□	320	◪		
■	321	◪		
	347			⧄
★	351			
⊙	368	◪		
⊙	415			
	433			⧄
⊠	434	◪		
⊠	436	◪		
2	437	◪		
◆	562	◪		
☆	597	◪		
%	598	◪		
	632			⧄
▼	640	◪		
▣	666	◪		
✕	725	◪		
⊡	726	⊡		
●	738	◪		
✕	754	◪		
⊠	758	◪		
▽	760	◪		
✳	761	◪		
⊙	762	◪		
▽	772	◪		
⊙	783	◪		
■	841	◪		
■	816	◪		
	924			⧄
⊙	926	◪	■	
■	927	◪	⊙	
−	928	◪	▲	
	931	⊡		⧄
⊡	948	◪		
✱	3021	◪		⧄ †
+	3072	◪		
=	3078	□		
⊙	3328	◪		⧄ †
★	3348	◪		
■	3371	◪		⧄ *
◇	3782	◪		
	3809			⧄
⊡	3810	◪		
●	433	French Knot		
●	3021	French Knot		
●	3371	French Knot		

* Use blanc for tree and work in long
  stitches. Use 3371 for all other.
† Use 3021 for hair, eyes, and
  eyebrows. Use 3328 for baby's
  mouth.

GOOD CHILDREN

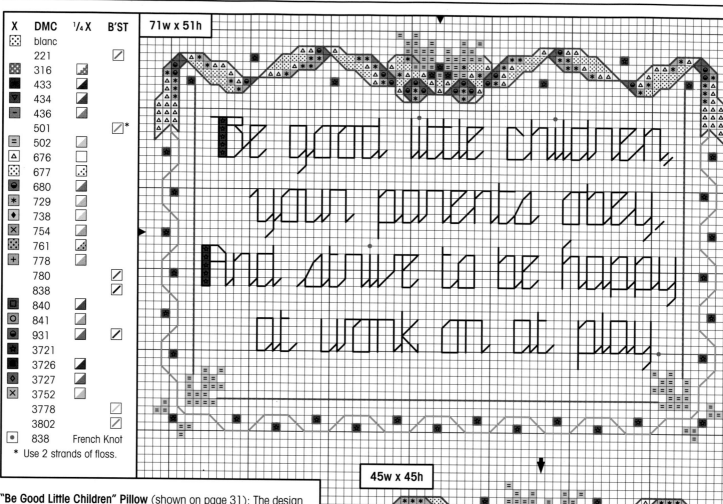

X	DMC	¼X	B'ST
▨	blanc		
	221		◪
▨	316	◪	
■	433	◪	
▽	434	◪	
⊡	436	◪	
	501		◪*
=	502	◪	
△	676	◪	
▨	677	◪	
◉	680	◪	
✱	729	◪	
◆	738	◪	
✕	754	◪	
▨	761	◪	
✚	778	◪	
	780		◪
	838		◪
▣	840	◪	
⊙	841	◪	
◉	931	◪	◪
✿	3721		
■	3726	◪	
◈	3727	◪	
✕	3752	◪	
	3778		◪
	3802		◪
●	838	French Knot	

* Use 2 strands of floss.

71w x 51h

"Be Good Little Children" Pillow (shown on page 31): The design was stitched over 2 fabric threads on an 8" x 7" piece of Cream Belfast Linen (32 ct). Two strands of floss were used for Cross Stitch and 1 strand for Backstitch and French Knots, unless otherwise noted in the color key.

For pillow, you will need a 7" x 5³/₄" piece of fabric for backing, 4" x 44" fabric strip for ruffle (pieced as necessary), 2" x 23¹/₂" bias fabric strip for cording, 23¹/₂" length of ¹/₄" dia. purchased cord, and polyester fiberfill.

Centering design, trim stitched piece to measure 7" x 5³/₄". To complete pillow, see Finishing Instructions, page 81.

"Baby's First Christmas" Ornament (shown on page 31): The design was stitched over 2 fabric threads on a 7" square of Cream Belfast Linen (32 ct). Two strands of floss were used for Cross Stitch and 1 strand for Backstitch, unless otherwise noted in the color key. Personalize and date ornament using alphabet and numerals provided.

For ornament, you will need a 4³/₄" x 4⁵/₈" piece of Cream Belfast Linen for backing, two 3³/₄" x 3⁵/₈" pieces of adhesive mounting board, two 3³/₄" x 3⁵/₈" pieces of batting, 2" x 17" bias fabric strip for cording, 17" length of ¹/₄" dia. purchased cord, and clear-drying craft glue.

Centering design, trim stitched piece to measure 4³/₄" x 4⁵/₈". To complete ornament, see Finishing Instructions, page 89.

Designs by Jane Chandler.

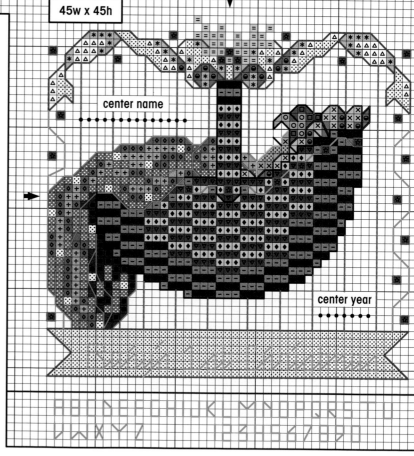

45w x 45h

center name

center year

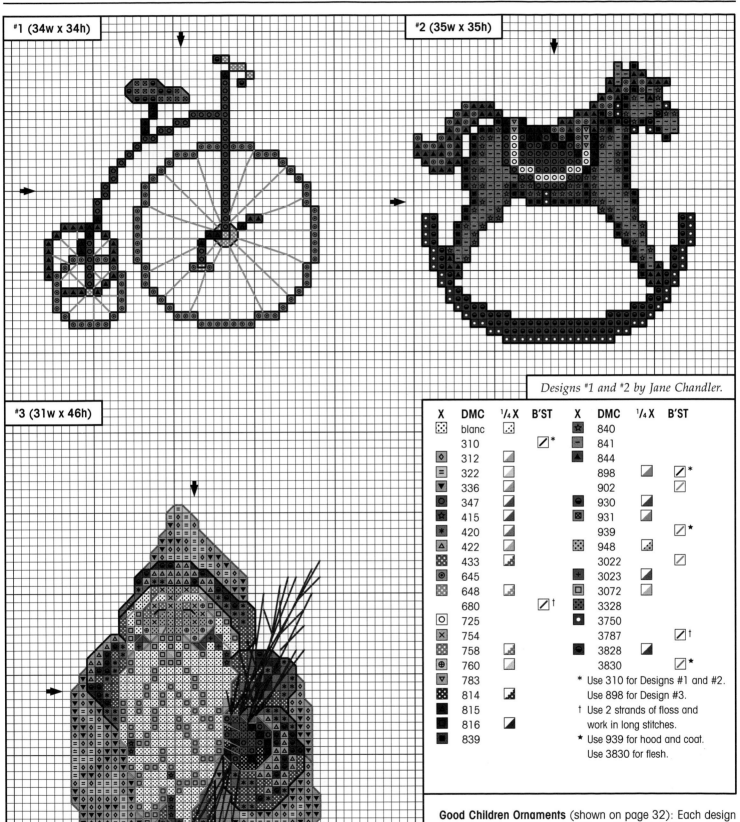

#1 (34w x 34h)

#2 (35w x 35h)

Designs #1 and #2 by Jane Chandler.

#3 (31w x 46h)

X	DMC	¼X	B'ST	X	DMC	¼X	B'ST
⊠	blanc	⊡		★	840		
	310		◪*	▦	841		
◇	312	◪		▲	844		
=	322	◪			898	◪	◪*
▼	336	◪			902		◪
⊙	347	◪		●	930	◪	
★	415	◪		⊠	931		
✳	420	◪			939		◪*
△	422	◪		⊠	948	◪	
⊠	433	◪			3022		◪
⊙	645			⊡	3023	◪	
⊠	648	◪		⊡	3072	◪	
	680		◪†	⊠	3328		
○	725			●	3750		
✕	754				3787		◪†
⊠	758	◪		⊞	3828	◪	
⊕	760	◪			3830		◪*
▽	783	◪					
⊠	814	◪					
■	815						
■	816	◪					
■	839						

* Use 310 for Designs #1 and #2.
Use 898 for Design #3.

† Use 2 strands of floss and
work in long stitches.

* Use 939 for hood and coat.
Use 3830 for flesh.

Good Children Ornaments (shown on page 32): Each design was stitched on an 8" square of Ivory Aida (14 ct). Three strands of floss were used for Cross Stitch and 1 strand for Backstitch, unless otherwise noted in the color key. They were inserted in purchased gold oval frames (3" x 4" opening).

Needlework adaptation by Jane Chandler.

GOOD CHILDREN

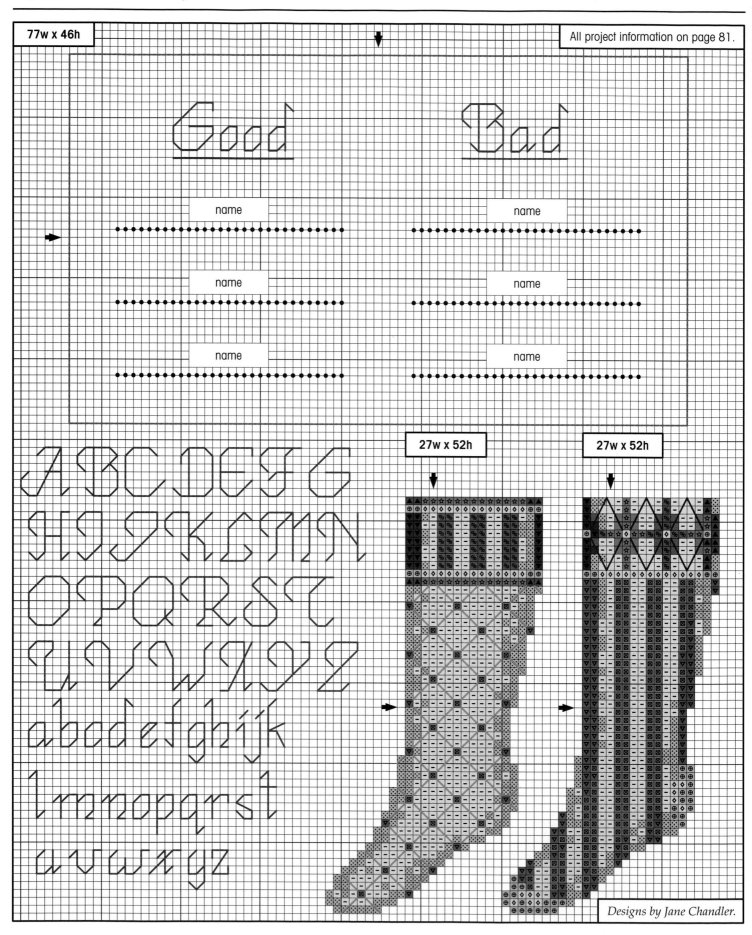

77w x 46h

All project information on page 81.

Good   Bad

name   name

name   name

name   name

27w x 52h   27w x 52h

Designs by Jane Chandler.

78

X	DMC	¼X	B'ST		X	DMC	¼X	B'ST
⊞	blanc	⊡			⊕	783	◪	◪
−	ecru	◪			■	815		
■	300				▣	822	◪	
✳	301				▨	842		
	310		◪		■	890	◪	◪
◆	312				◕	915		◪
▽	319		◪		▽	917		◪
◆	321	◪	◪		▲	930		
▣	322	◪			☆	931		
▨	347					3345	◪	
⊠	367				◇	3346		
◉	400				○	3347		
▧	434	◪			+	3371		◪
◉	435	◪	◪		+	3755	◪	
☆	437	◪			−	3776		
▩	498	◪			☐	blanc		French Knot
◆	642	◪			•	3371		French Knot
✳	644	◪			◪			Indicates cutting line.
2	666				☐*			* Work in long stitches.
⊙	676	◪						
✕	677	◪						
▦	680	◪						
◇	725	◪	☐*					
•	727	•						
★	729	◪						

STITCH COUNT (64w x 101h)

14 count	4⁵⁄₈"	x	7¼"
16 count	4"	x	6³⁄₈"
18 count	3⁵⁄₈"	x	5⁵⁄₈"
22 count	3"	x	4⁵⁄₈"

Trimmed Tree Afghan (shown on page 33): The design was stitched over 2 fabric threads on a 45" x 58" piece of Ivory All-Cotton Anne Cloth (18 ct).

For afghan, cut off selvages of fabric; measure 5½" from raw edge of fabric and pull out 1 fabric thread. Fringe fabric up to missing fabric thread. Repeat for each side. Tie an overhand knot at each corner with 4 horizontal and 4 vertical fabric threads. Working from corners, use 8 fabric threads for each knot until all threads are knotted.

Refer to Diagram for placement of design on fabric; use 6 strands of floss for Cross Stitch and 2 strands for Backstitch and French Knots.

For bead garlands, you will need Mill Hill Beads - 02013 and nylon thread. String beads on five lengths of nylon thread; referring to photo for placement, secure ends of each bead garland on wrong side of afghan and tack in place as desired.

Diagram

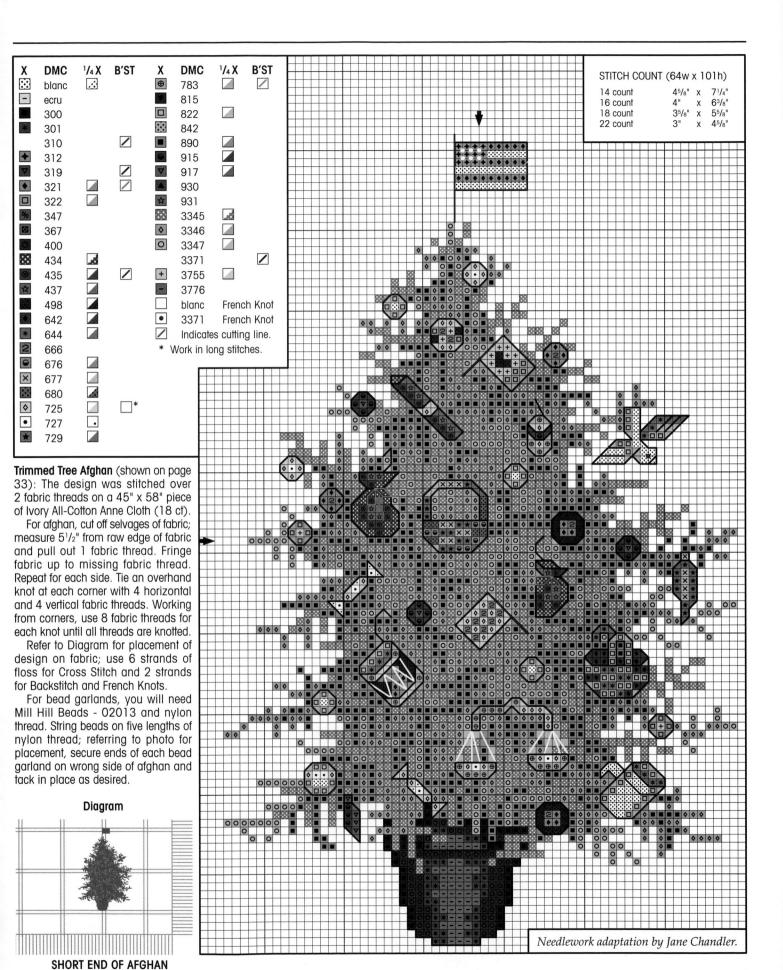

Needlework adaptation by Jane Chandler.

SHORT END OF AFGHAN

CHRISTMAS GUARDIAN

STITCH COUNT (66w x 107h)

14 count	4³/₄"	x 7³/₄"
16 count	4¹/₈"	x 6³/₄"
18 count	3³/₄"	x 6"
22 count	3"	x 4⁷/₈"

Christmas Guardian in Frame (shown on page 35): The design was stitched over 2 fabric threads on a 13" x 16" piece of Antique White Cashel Linen (28 ct). Three strands of floss were used for Cross Stitch and 1 strand for Half Cross Stitch and Backstitch. It was custom framed.

Needlework adaptation by Donna Vermillion Giampa.

X	DMC	1/4 X	1/2 X	B'ST	X	DMC	1/4 X	1/2 X	B'ST	X	DMC	1/4 X	1/2 X	B'ST	X	DMC	1/4 X	1/2 X	B'ST
✓	blanc	✓		✓*	✓	729	✓			✓	890	✓		✓†		3768			✓▲
✓	309	✓				738		✓		✓	899	✓			✓	3770		✓	
✓	321	✓				739		✓			902			✓*	✓	3772 &	✓		
✓	326	✓		✓*		746		✓		✓*	926 &		✓			blanc			
✓	335	✓				747		✓			841				✓	3773		✓	
✓	407	✓			✓	761	✓			✓*	927 &		✓		✓*	3773 &	✓		
	414		✓		✓	762		✓			842					blanc			
✓	415	✓			✓	816		✓		✓	928				✓	3774		✓	
✓	433			✓†		818		✓			931	✓				3810		✓	
	436	✓			✓	839	✓			✓	950	✓				3830			✓▲
	437	✓			✓*	839 &		✓		✓*	950 &								
✓	543					blanc					blanc								
	597	✓			✓	840		✓			3031			✓					
	598	✓			✓*	840 &	✓			✓	3045	✓							
	632		✓			blanc				✓	3046	✓							
✓	666	✓			✓	841		✓		✓	3047	✓							
✓	676	✓			✓*	841 &				✓	3326	✓							
✓	677	✓				blanc				✓	3345	✓							
✓	680	✓			✓	842				✓	3347								
✓	702	✓				869			✓	✓	3756	✓							

* Use blanc for stars. Use 326 for dress. Use 902 for buildings.

† Use 433 for floor. Use 890 for trees.

★ Use 2 strands of first floss color listed and 1 strand of second floss color listed.

▲ Use 3768 for clothing. Use 3830 for mouths.

FINISHING INSTRUCTIONS

"Merry Christmas to All" Pillow (shown on page 8, chart and supplies on pages 56-57) and **"Be Good Little Children" Pillow** (shown on page 31, chart and supplies on page 76): Center cord on wrong side of bias strip; matching long edges, fold strip over cord. Use a zipper foot to baste along length of strip close to cord; trim seam allowance to 1/2". Matching raw edges, pin cording to right side of stitched piece, making a 3/8" clip in seam allowance of cording at corners. Ends of cording should overlap approximately 2"; pin overlapping end out of the way. Starting 2" from beginning end of cording and ending 4" from overlapping end, baste cording to stitched piece. On overlapping end of cording, remove 2 1/2" of basting; fold end of fabric back and trim cord so that it meets beginning end of cord. Fold end of fabric 1/2" to wrong side; wrap fabric over beginning end of cording. Finish basting cording to stitched piece.

For ruffle, press short edges of fabric strip 1/2" to wrong side. Matching wrong sides and long edges, fold strip in half; press. Machine baste 1/2" from raw edges; gather fabric strip to fit stitched piece. Matching raw edges, pin ruffle to right side of stitched piece, overlapping short ends 1/4". Use a 1/2" seam allowance to sew ruffle to stitched piece.

Matching right sides and leaving an opening for turning, use a 1/2" seam allowance to sew stitched piece and backing fabric together. Trim seam allowances diagonally at corners; turn pillow right side out, carefully pushing corners outward. Stuff pillow with polyester fiberfill and blind stitch opening closed.

Stocking Ornaments (shown on page 32, charts on page 78): Each design was stitched on a 4" x 6" piece of Ivory Aida (14 ct). Three strands of floss were used for Cross Stitch and 1 strand for Backstitch.

For each ornament, you will need a 4" x 6" piece of Ivory Aida for backing. Matching right sides and raw edges, place stitched piece and backing fabric together. Using a zipper foot and backstitching at beginning and end of seam, start 3/4" above top edge of design (leave top edge open) and sew fabric pieces together 1/8" away from design. Trim top edge 3/4" from design

and trim seam allowance to 1/4"; clip curves and turn ornament right side out. Turn top edge of ornament 1/4" to wrong side and press; turn 3/8" to wrong side and hem.

St. Nick's List Ornament (shown on page 32): Using alphabet, page 78, and referring to photo, stitch desired names on a 4" x 10" piece of Ivory Aida (18 ct). One strand of floss was used for Backstitch.

For ornament, you will need a 4" x 10" piece of lightweight cream fabric for backing, fabric stiffener, and small foam brush. Apply a heavy coat of fabric stiffener to back of stitched piece using small foam brush. Matching wrong sides, place stitched piece on backing fabric, smoothing stitched piece while pressing fabric pieces together; allow to dry. Apply fabric stiffener to backing fabric; allow to dry. Trim stiffened piece, allowing 2 3/4" margins at top and bottom and 1/2" margins at sides. Referring to photo, curl short ends of ornament.

Book Ornament (shown on page 32, chart on page 78): The design was stitched on a 6" x 4 1/2" piece of Ivory Aida (18 ct). One strand of floss was used for Backstitch. Referring to photo, use alphabet to personalize ornament.

For ornament, you will need a 6" x 4 1/2" piece of lightweight cream fabric for stitched piece backing, 4 1/2" x 3" piece of Black Aida, a 4 1/2" x 3" piece of lightweight black fabric for backing, fabric stiffener, small foam brush, clear-drying craft glue, and a 4" length of 1/16"w ribbon for bookmark.

Apply a heavy coat of fabric stiffener to back of stitched piece using small foam brush. Matching wrong sides, place stitched piece on cream backing fabric, smoothing stitched piece while pressing fabric pieces together; allow to dry. Apply fabric stiffener to backing fabric; allow to dry. Repeat with Black Aida and black backing fabric.

Centering design, trim stiffened cream piece to 4 1/4" x 2 1/2". Referring to photo, shape stiffened cream piece and glue center and short edges to stiffened Black Aida. For bookmark, referring to photo, glue ribbon to ornament.

woodland christmas

X	DMC	¼X	½X	B'ST
⊡	blanc	⊡		
▨	349	◪		
▲	351	◪		
▪	352	◪		
▼	355	◪		◪*
◉	422	◪		
	632			◪*
★	640	◪		◪*
◎	642	◪		
▨	644	◪		
▽	760	◪		
≡	761			
■	815	◪		
◆	817	◪		
◈	822	▢		
	869			◪†
	895			◪
	902			◪
▨	928	◪		
◆	930			◪
✳	931			
✕	950	◪		
▲	3021	◪		
	3031			◪†
▢	3045			
➕	3047			
✕	3072	◪		
■	3345	◪		
▨	3346	◪		
▬	3347	◪		
◈	3348	◪		
◇	3770	▢		
■	3772	◪		
▨	3773	◪		
⊡	3774	◪		
▪	3787			◪
	3817		▢	
⊙	blanc		French Knot	
⊙	3031		French Knot	

* Use 355 for mouth. Use 632
for flesh. Use 640 for branches.
† Use 869 for strap. Use 3031 for
bird and eyes.

STITCH COUNT (57w x 84h)

14 count	4⅛"	x	6"
16 count	3⅝"	x	5¼"
18 count	3¼"	x	4¾"
22 count	2⅝"	x	3⅞"

Gentle Santa with Bird in Frame
(shown on page 38): The design
was stitched on a 12" x 14" piece
of Fiddler's Lite (14 ct). Three strands
of floss were used for Cross Stitch
and 1 strand for Half Cross Stitch,
Backstitch, and French Knots. It was
inserted in a purchased frame
(5" x 7" opening) and attached to a
decorated 13" dia. grapevine wreath.

*Needlework adaptation by
Donna Vermillion Giampa.*

X	DMC	1/4X	1/2X	B'ST
⁘	blanc	⁘		
	347			∕*
▣	353	◢		
	356			∕*
■	433	◢		∕
▲	434	◢		
◆	501	◢		
▲	502			
	646		−	∕
	647		★	
	648		■	
⁘	676	⁘		
■	677	◢	★	
★	725	◢		
◎	729	◢		
	743		■	
⁘	744	⁘		∕†
−	745	◻		
	792		■	
	793		◎	
	794		▽	
⊠	822			
=	869			∕
	898			∕★
	928		⊠	
	938			∕★
▼	945	◢		
⁘	951	⁘		
*	3024	◢		
⊖	3041			
◆	3042			
	3072		⊖	
■	3362			
○	3363			
+	3740	◢		
	3773	◢		
▽	3813			
⁘	3829	◢		

* Use 347 for robe. Use 356 for flesh.

† Use 1 strand of floss and 1 strand of Kreinik Blending Filament - 002.

★ Use 898 for hair, eyes, and eyebrows. Use 938 for robe.

STITCH COUNT (54w x 90h)
14 count 3⅞" x 6½"
16 count 3⅜" x 5⅝"
18 count 3" x 5"
22 count 2½" x 4⅛"
Needlework adaptation by Nancy Dockter.

Adoring the Christ Child in Frame (shown on page 37): The design was stitched on an 11" x 14" piece of Fiddler's Lite (16 ct). Two strands of floss were used for Cross Stitch and 1 strand for Half Cross Stitch and Backstitch, unless otherwise noted in the color key. It was inserted in a twig-covered frame.

For frame, you will need a purchased frame with 2" wide molding (5" x 7" opening), twigs cut to approximately 2" lengths, and clear-drying craft glue. Referring to photo, glue twigs to frame.

woodland christmas

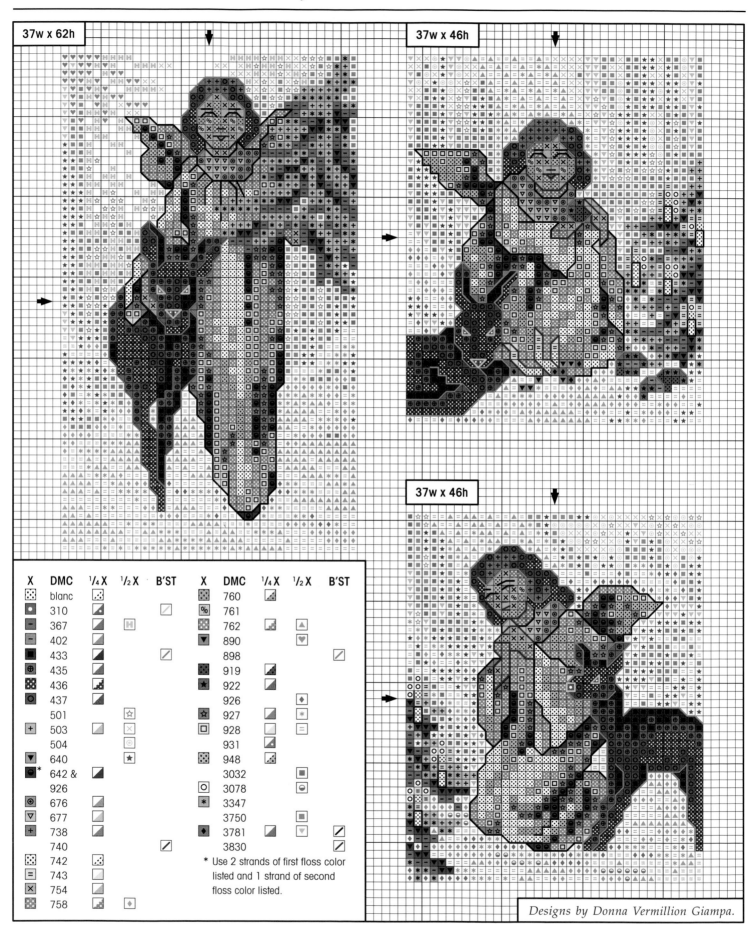

X	DMC	¼ X	½ X	B'ST	X	DMC	¼ X	½ X	B'ST
	blanc					760			
	310				%	761			
-	367		H			762			
-	402				▼	890			
■	433					898			
⊕	435					919			
▨	436				★	922			
○	437					926			
	501	☆				927			
+	503		✕		□	928			
	504		⊙			931			
▼	640		★			948			
▣*	642 &					3032		■	
	926				○	3078		⊟	
⊙	676				✳	3347			
▽	677					3750		■	
+	738				◆	3781		▼	
	740					3830			
▨	742				* Use 2 strands of first floss color				
=	743				listed and 1 strand of second				
✕	754				floss color listed.				
▨	758		⊡						

37w x 62h

37w x 46h

37w x 46h

Designs by Donna Vermillion Giampa.

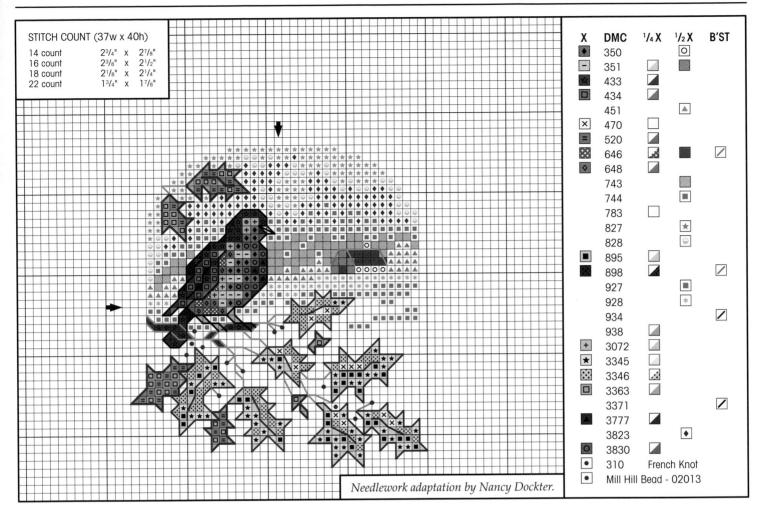

STITCH COUNT (37w x 40h)

count	width	height
14 count	2¾"	2⅞"
16 count	2⅜"	2½"
18 count	2⅛"	2¼"
22 count	1¾"	1⅞"

X	DMC	¼ X	½ X	B'ST
◆	350		○	
−	351	◹	▨	
★	433		◪	
▣	434		◪	
	451		▲	
✕	470	□		
=	520		◪	
▨	646	◪	■	╱
◈	648		◪	
	743		■	
	744		■	
	783	□		
	827		★	
	828		◉	
■	895	◹		
■	898	◪		╱
	927		■	
	928		✳	
	934			╱
	938	◹		
+	3072	◹		
★	3345	□		
▨	3346	⬚		
▣	3363	◹		
	3371			╱
■	3777	◪		
	3823		◆	
◎	3830	◹		
●	310	French Knot		
●	Mill Hill Bead - 02013			

Needlework adaptation by Nancy Dockter.

Woodland Angel Ornaments (shown on page 39): Each design was stitched on a 7" x 8" piece of Fiddler's Lite (14 ct). Three strands of floss were used for Cross Stitch and 1 strand for Half Cross Stitch and Backstitch.

For each ornament, you will need a 7" x 8" piece of lightweight cream fabric for backing, fabric stiffener, small foam brush, adhesive mounting board, assorted twigs, clear-drying craft glue, and 6" length of jute twine.

Apply a heavy coat of fabric stiffener to wrong side of stitched piece using small foam brush. Matching wrong sides, place stitched piece on backing fabric, smoothing stitched piece while pressing fabric pieces together; allow to dry. Apply fabric stiffener to backing fabric; allow to dry.

Trim each stiffened piece two squares away from edge of design. Cut a piece of adhesive mounting board the same size as stiffened piece. Remove paper from adhesive mounting board and center on wrong side of stiffened piece. Cut two twigs approximately 1½" longer than the height of stiffened piece. Referring to photo, center twigs on long edges of stiffened piece. Glue twigs in place; allow to dry. Cut two twigs approximately 1½" longer than the width of stiffened piece. Referring to photo, center twigs on short edges of stiffened piece. Glue to vertical twigs; allow to dry.

For hanger, refer to photo and glue ends of jute to wrong side of ornament.

Songbird Ornament (shown on page 38): The design was stitched on a 7" square of Fiddler's Lite (14 ct). Three strands of floss were used for Cross Stitch and 1 strand for Half Cross Stitch, Backstitch, and French Knot. Attach beads using 1 strand of DMC 498 floss; see Attaching Beads below.

For ornament, you will need a 5" dia. grapevine wreath, 7" square of lightweight cream fabric for backing, clear-drying craft glue, fabric stiffener, and small foam brush.

Apply a heavy coat of fabric stiffener to back of stitched piece using small foam brush. Matching wrong sides, place stitched piece on backing fabric, smoothing stitched piece while pressing fabric pieces together; allow to dry. Apply fabric stiffener to backing fabric; allow to dry. Centering design, trim stiffened piece to a 4¾" dia. circle; referring to photo, glue to back of wreath.

ATTACHING BEADS

Refer to chart for bead placement and sew bead in place using a fine needle that will pass through bead. Bring needle up at 1, run needle through bead, then down at 2, making a Half Cross Stitch (**Fig. 1**). Secure floss on back or move to next bead as shown in **Fig. 1**.

Fig. 1

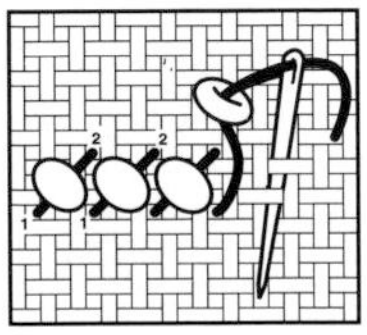

A FINE CHRISTMAS SNOW MAN

STITCH COUNT (69w x 96h)

14 count	5"	x	6⅞"
16 count	4⅜"	x	6"
18 count	3⅞"	x	5⅜"
22 count	3¼"	x	4⅜"

X	DMC	¼ X	½ X	B'ST
	blanc			
	310			⁄ *
	319			
	347			
	350			
	351			
	353			
†	353 & 3708			
	356			⁄
	500			
	517			
X	644			
	646			
=	648			
	680			
	729			
X	747			
-	758			
	760			
★	806			
◇	807			
	814			
	816			
◇	822			
	824			
▲	844			
▲	869			⁄ *
☆	987			
	3023			
	3031			⁄ *
○	3072			
-	3347			
	3348			
	3371			⁄
□	3766			
	3799			⁄
◆	3820			
+	3821			
◉	3829			⁄ *
	3830			⁄
⚫	blanc	French Knot		
●	310	French Knot		

* Use 310 for snowman. Use 869 for hair. Use 3031 for girls' eyes. Use 3829 for flower center.

† Use 2 strands of first floss color listed and 1 strand of second floss color listed.

A Fine Christmas Snow Man in Frame (shown on page 41): The design was stitched over 2 fabric threads on a 14" x 16" piece of Antique White Lugana (25 ct). Three strands of floss were used for Cross Stitch and 1 strand for Half Cross Stitch, Backstitch, and French Knots. It was custom framed.

Needlework adaptation by Nancy Dockter.

LETTERS SANTA LIKES

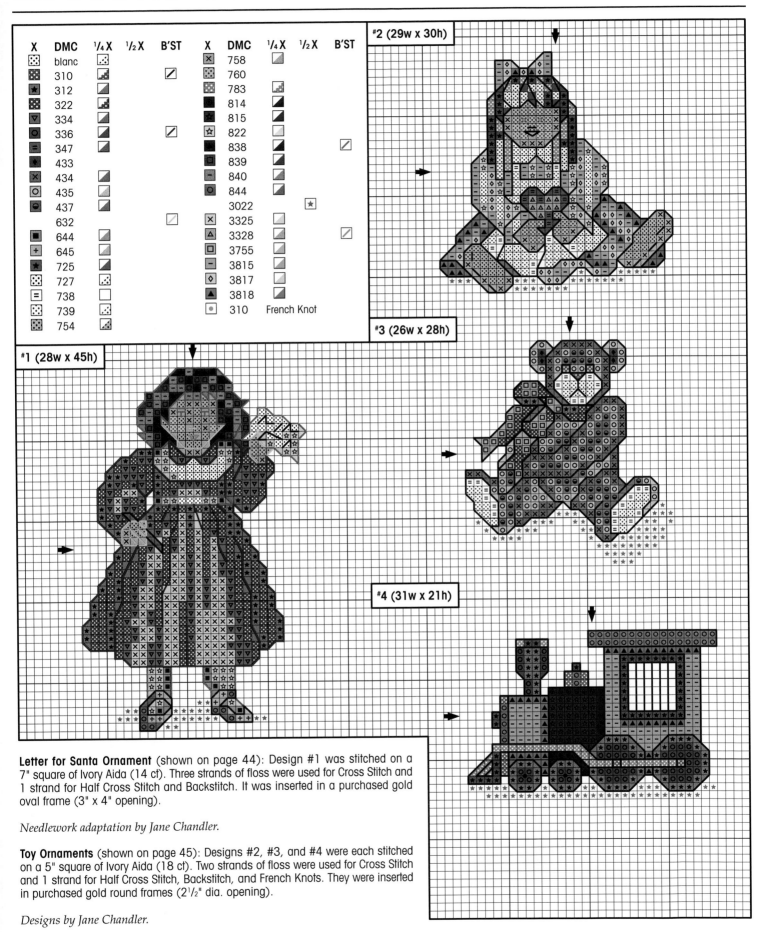

X	DMC	¼ X	½ X	B'ST		X	DMC	¼ X	½ X	B'ST
	blanc					X	758			
	310			/			760			
★	312						783			
	322						814			
▽	334						815			
○	336			/		☆	822			
▤	347						838			/
★	433						839			
✕	434						840			
○	435					●	844			
●	437						3022			
	632			/		✕	3325			
■	644					△	3328			/
+	645					▢	3755			
★	725					–	3815			
▨	727					◇	3817			
=	738					▲	3818			
▨	739					•	310			French Knot
▨	754									

#2 (29w x 30h)

#3 (26w x 28h)

#1 (28w x 45h)

#4 (31w x 21h)

Letter for Santa Ornament (shown on page 44): Design #1 was stitched on a 7" square of Ivory Aida (14 ct). Three strands of floss were used for Cross Stitch and 1 strand for Half Cross Stitch and Backstitch. It was inserted in a purchased gold oval frame (3" x 4" opening).

Needlework adaptation by Jane Chandler.

Toy Ornaments (shown on page 45): Designs #2, #3, and #4 were each stitched on a 5" square of Ivory Aida (18 ct). Two strands of floss were used for Cross Stitch and 1 strand for Half Cross Stitch, Backstitch, and French Knots. They were inserted in purchased gold round frames (2½" dia. opening).

Designs by Jane Chandler.

LETTERS SANTA LIKES

STITCH COUNT (84w x 56h)			
14 count	6"	x	4"
16 count	5¼"	x	3½"
18 count	4¾"	x	3⅛"
22 count	3⅞"	x	2⅝"

"Hello Little One" Hanging Pillow (shown on page 44): The design was stitched on a 12" x 10" piece of Ivory Aida (14 ct). Three strands of floss were used for Cross Stitch and 1 strand for Backstitch and French Knots.

For pillow, you will need 7¾" x 5¾" piece of lightweight fabric for backing, 2" x 26" bias fabric strip for cording, 26" length of ¼" dia. purchased cord, two 18" lengths of ⅝"w ribbon for hanger, and polyester fiberfill.

Centering design, trim stitched piece to measure 7¾" x 5¾".

For cording, center cord on wrong side of bias strip; matching long edges, fold strip over cord. Use a zipper foot to baste along length of strip close to cord; trim seam allowance to ½". Matching raw edges, pin cording to right side of stitched piece, making a ⅜" clip in seam allowance of cording at corners. Ends of cording should overlap approximately 2"; pin overlapping end out of the way. Starting 1" from beginning end of cording and ending 2½" from overlapping end, baste cording to stitched piece. On overlapping end of cording, remove 2" of basting; fold end of fabric back and trim cord so that it meets beginning end of cord. Fold end of fabric ½" to wrong side; wrap fabric over beginning end of cording. Finish basting cording to stitched piece.

Matching right sides and leaving an opening for turning, use a ½" seam allowance to sew stitched piece and backing fabric together. Trim seam allowances diagonally at corners; turn pillow right side out, carefully pushing corners outward. Stuff pillow with polyester fiberfill and blind stitch opening closed.

For hanger, refer to photo and tack one length of ribbon to each upper corner of pillow back. Trim ends and tie hanger in a bow.

"Dear Santa" Ornaments (shown on page 45): Each design was stitched on a 6" x 7" piece of Ivory Aida (16 ct). One strand of floss was used for Backstitch and French Knots.

For each ornament, you will need a 4⅝" x 5⅜" piece of Ivory Aida for backing, two 3⅛" x 3⅞" pieces of adhesive mounting board, two 3⅛" x 3⅞" pieces of batting, 2" x 18" bias fabric strip for cording, 18" length of ¼" dia. purchased cord, and clear-drying craft glue.

Centering design, trim stitched piece to measure 4⅝" x 5⅜". To complete ornament, see Finishing Instructions, page 89.

Designs by Jane Chandler.

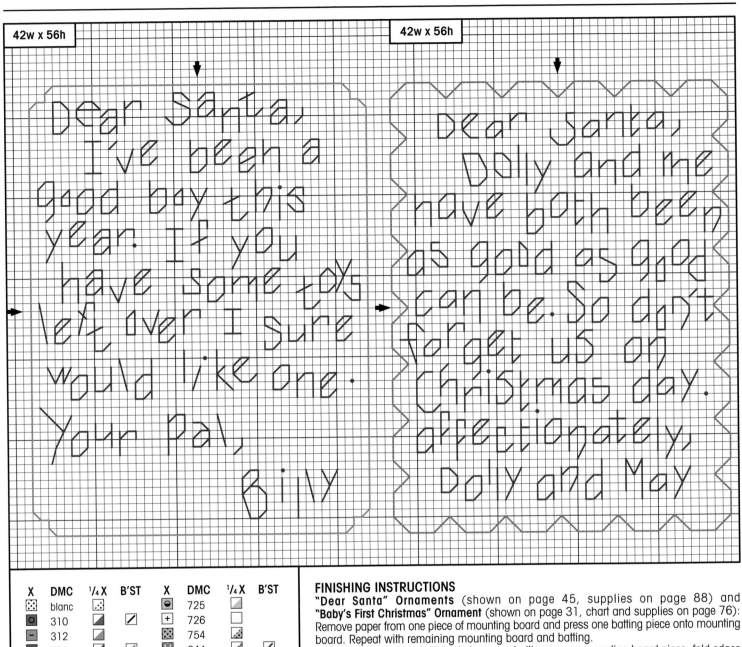

X	DMC	¼X	B'ST	X	DMC	¼X	B'ST
⊡	blanc	⊡		⊖	725	◪	
⊙	310	◪	╱	+	726	▨	
⊟	312	◪		⊞	754	◪	
▽	322	◪	╱	⊞	844	◪	╱
▤	347	◪	╱	◼	947	◪	
★	498	◪		▲	971	◪	
☆	550	◪			3328		╱
◉	552	◪		▣	3776	◪	
▲	612	◪		✕	3815	◪	
✚	646	◪		⊝	3818	◪	╱
◇	647	◪		•	310		French Knot
☆	676	◪		•	844		French Knot

FINISHING INSTRUCTIONS

"Dear Santa" Ornaments (shown on page 45, supplies on page 88) and "Baby's First Christmas" Ornament (shown on page 31, chart and supplies on page 76): Remove paper from one piece of mounting board and press one batting piece onto mounting board. Repeat with remaining mounting board and batting.

Center wrong side of stitched piece over batting on one mounting board piece; fold edges of stitched piece to back of mounting board and glue in place. For ornament back, repeat with backing fabric and remaining mounting board.

For cording, center cord on wrong side of bias strip; matching long edges, fold strip over cord. Use a zipper foot to baste along length of strip close to cord; trim seam allowance to ½". Starting at bottom center of stitched piece and 1½" from beginning of cording, glue cording seam allowance to wrong side of ornament front; stop 3" from overlapping end of cording. Ends of cording should overlap approximately 2". On overlapping end of cording, remove 2½" of basting; fold end of bias strip back and trim cord so that it meets beginning end of cord. Fold end of bias strip ½" to wrong side; wrap bias strip over beginning end of cording. Finish gluing cording to stitched piece. Matching wrong sides, glue ornament front and back together.

LETTERS SANTA LIKES

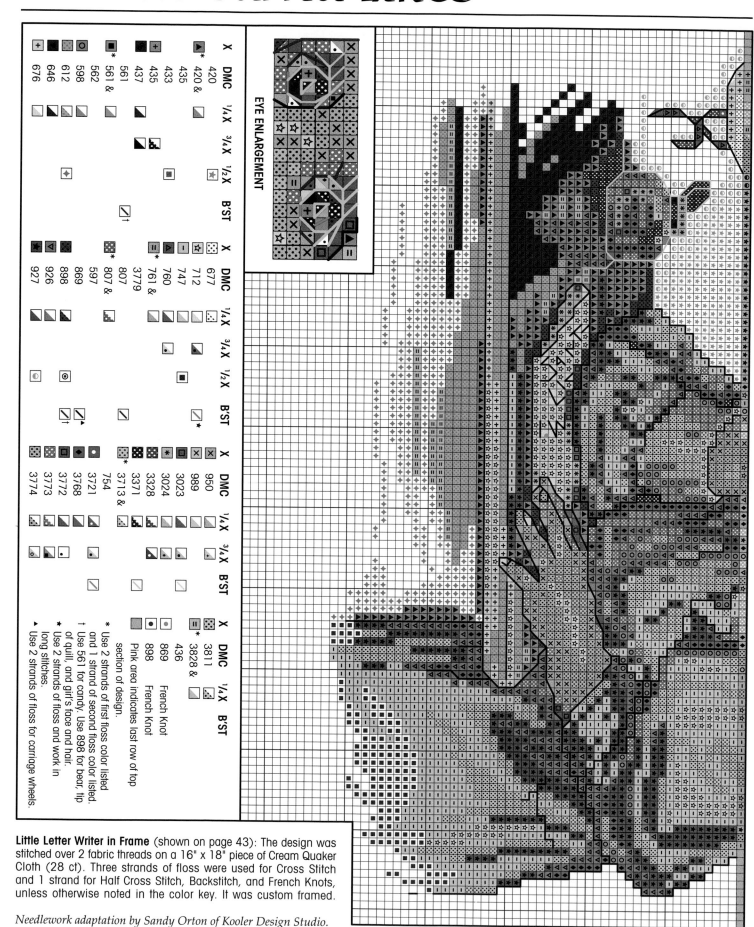

EYE ENLARGEMENT

X	¼X	¾X	½X	B'ST	DMC
					420
			★		420 &
					435
					433
					435
					437
					561
				†	561 &
					562
					598
					612
					646
					676

X	¼X	¾X	½X	B'ST	DMC
					677
					712
					747
					760
					761 &
					3779
					807
					807 &
					597
					869
					898
					926
					927

X	¼X	¾X	½X	B'ST	DMC
					950
					989
					3023
					3024
					3328
					3371
					3713 &
					3721
					754
					3768
					3772
					3773
					3774

X	¼X	¾X	B'ST	DMC	
				436	
				869	French Knot
				898	French Knot
				3811	
				3828 &	

Pink area indicates last row of top section of design.

* Use 2 strands of first floss color listed and 1 strand of second floss color listed.

† Use 561 for candy. Use 898 for bear, tip of quill, and girl's face and hair.

★ Use 2 strands of floss and work in long stitches.

▶ Use 2 strands of floss for carriage wheels.

Little Letter Writer in Frame (shown on page 43): The design was stitched over 2 fabric threads on a 16" x 18" piece of Cream Quaker Cloth (28 ct). Three strands of floss were used for Cross Stitch and 1 strand for Half Cross Stitch, Backstitch, and French Knots, unless otherwise noted in the color key. It was custom framed.

Needlework adaptation by Sandy Orton of Kooler Design Studio.

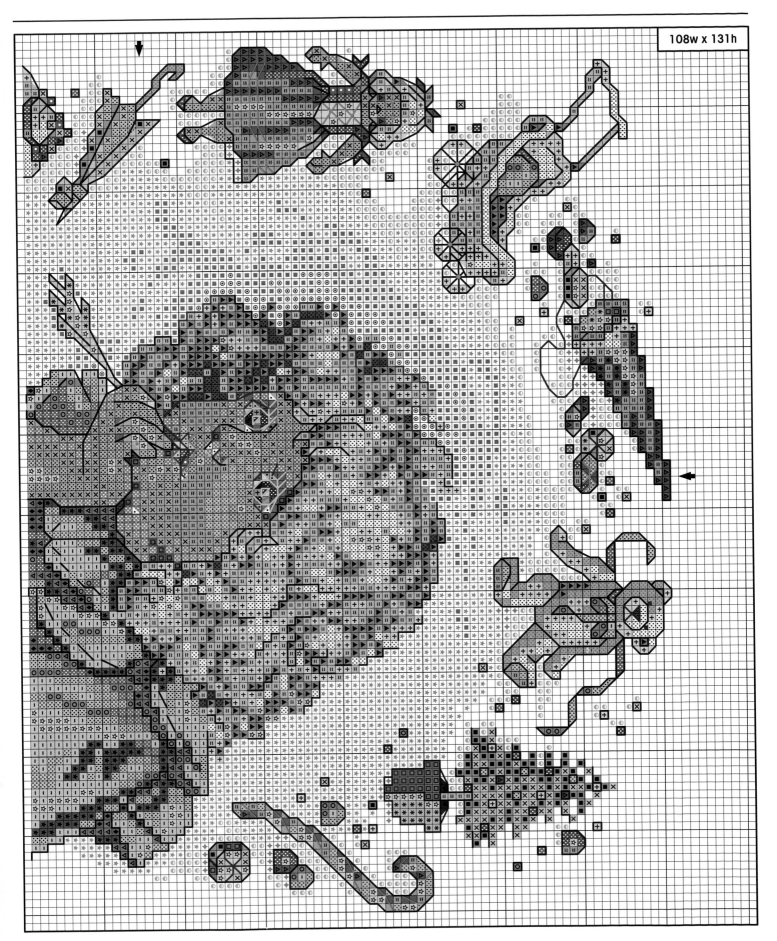

LONG MAY HE LIVE!

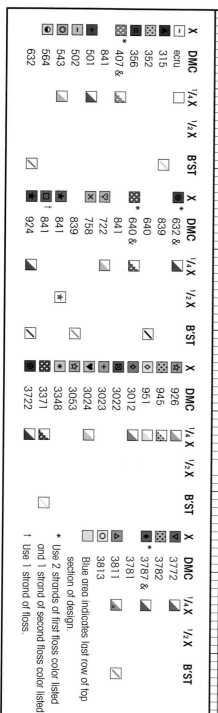

X						DMC	¼X	½X	B'ST
-						ecru			
						315			
						352			
						356			
*						407 &			
						841			
						501			
						502			
						543			
						564			
						632			

X	*					DMC	¼X	½X	B'ST
						632 &			
						839			
						640			
						640 &	*		
						841			
						722			
						758			
						839			
						841			
						924			

X	⊙					DMC	¼X	½X	B'ST
						926			
						945			
						951			
						3012			
						3022			
						3023			
						3024			
						3053			
						3348			
						3371			
						3722			

X	*					DMC	¼X	½X	B'ST
						3772			
						3782			
						3787 &			
						3781			
						3811			
						3813			

Blue area indicates last row of top
section of design.

* Use 2 strands of first floss color listed
and 1 strand of second floss color listed.

† Use 1 strand of floss.

Long May He Live in Frame (shown on page 49): The design was stitched over 2 fabric threads on a 15" x 19" piece of Light Mocha Cashel Linen (28 ct). Three strands of floss were used for Cross Stitch and 1 strand for Half Cross Stitch and Backstitch, unless otherwise noted in the color key. It was custom framed.

*Needlework adaptation by
Sandy Orton of Kooler Design Studio.*

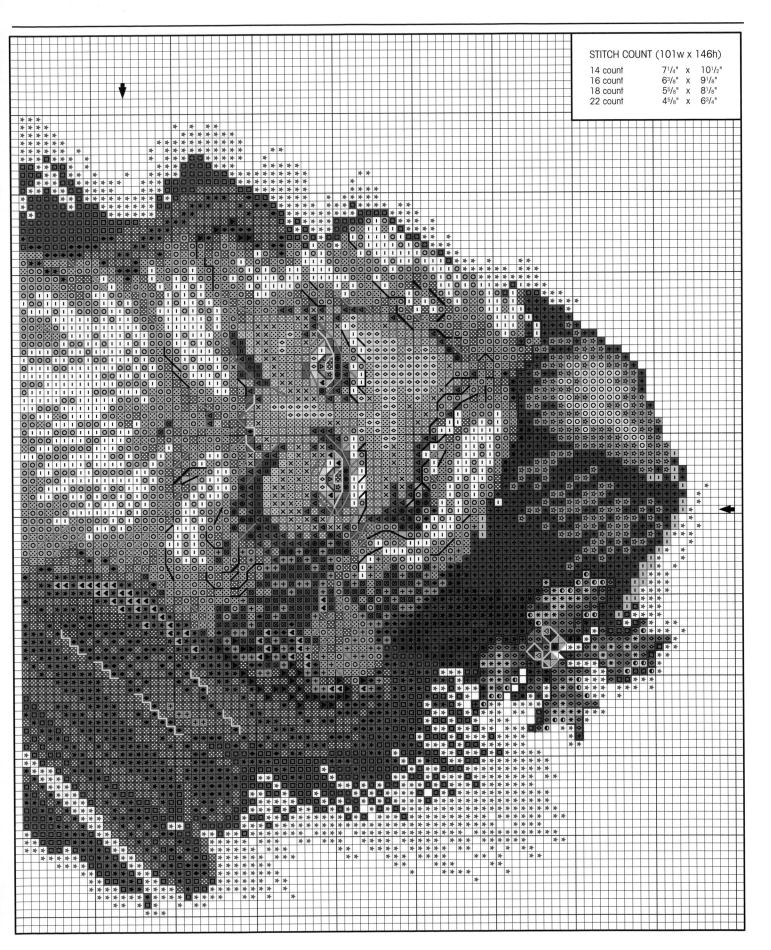

STITCH COUNT (101w x 146h)

14 count	7¼"	x	10½"
16 count	6³/₈"	x	9¹/₈"
18 count	5⁵/₈"	x	8¹/₈"
22 count	4⁵/₈"	x	6³/₄"

children's chorus

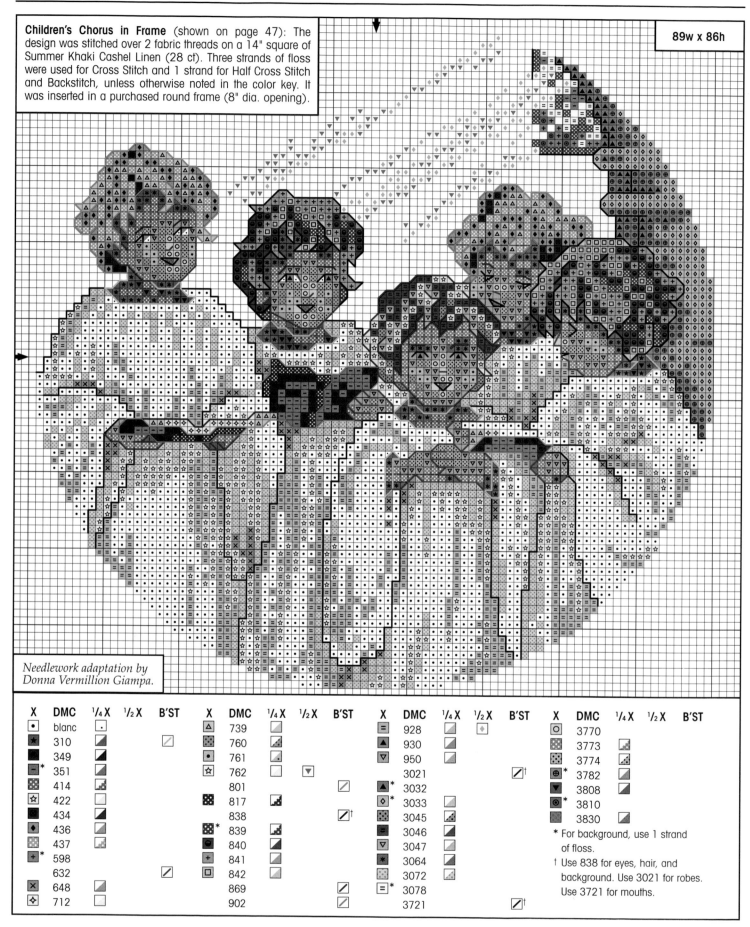

Children's Chorus in Frame (shown on page 47): The design was stitched over 2 fabric threads on a 14" square of Summer Khaki Cashel Linen (28 ct). Three strands of floss were used for Cross Stitch and 1 strand for Half Cross Stitch and Backstitch, unless otherwise noted in the color key. It was inserted in a purchased round frame (8" dia. opening).

89w x 86h

Needlework adaptation by Donna Vermillion Giampa.

X	DMC	¼X	½X	B'ST	X	DMC	¼X	½X	B'ST	X	DMC	¼X	½X	B'ST	X	DMC	¼X	½X	B'ST
•	blanc				▲	739				=	928		◆		○	3770			
★	310					760				▲	930					3773			
	349				•	761				▽	950					3774			
— *	351				☆	762		▽			3021				⊕ *	3782			
	414					801				▲ *	3032				▼	3808			
☆	422					817				◇ *	3033				⊙ *	3810			
	434					838					3045					3830			
◆	436				*	839				=	3046								
	437					840				▽	3047								
+ *	598				+	841				*	3064								
	632				□	842					3072								
✕	648					869				= *	3078								
◆	712					902					3721								

* For background, use 1 strand of floss.

† Use 838 for eyes, hair, and background. Use 3021 for robes. Use 3721 for mouths.

94

GENERAL INSTRUCTIONS

WORKING WITH CHARTS

How to Read Charts: Each of the designs is shown in chart form. Each colored square on the chart represents one Cross Stitch or one Half Cross Stitch. Each colored triangle on the chart represents one One-Quarter Stitch or one Three-Quarter Stitch. In some charts, reduced symbols are used to indicate One-Quarter Stitches and Three-Quarter Stitches (**Fig. 1**). **Fig. 2** and **Fig. 3** indicate Cross Stitch under Backstitch.

Fig. 1   **Fig. 2**   **Fig. 3**

Colored dots on the chart represent French Knots or bead placement. The black or colored straight lines on the chart indicate Backstitch. When a French Knot or Backstitch covers a square, the symbol is omitted or reduced.

Each chart is accompanied by a color key. This key indicates the color of floss to use for each stitch on the chart. The headings on the color key are for Cross Stitch (**X**), DMC color number (**DMC**), One-Quarter Stitch (**¼X**), Three-Quarter Stitch (**¾X**), Half Cross Stitch (**½X**), and Backstitch (**B'ST**). Color key columns should be read vertically and horizontally to determine type of stitch and floss color. Some designs may include stitches worked with metallic thread, such as Blending Filament or Braid. The metallic thread may be blended with floss or used alone. If any metallic thread is used in a design, the color key will contain the necessary information.

Where to Start: The horizontal and vertical centers of each charted design are shown by arrows. You may start at any point on the charted design, but be sure the design will be centered on the fabric. Locate the center of fabric by folding in half from top to bottom and again left to right. On the charted design, count the number of squares (stitches) from the center of the chart to where you wish to start. Then, from the fabric's center, find your starting point by counting out the same number of fabric threads (stitches). (**Note:** To work over two fabric threads, count out twice the number of fabric threads.)

Instructions tested and photo items made by Marsha Besancon, Vicky Bishop, Margaret Bredlow, Elaine Garrett, Muriel Hicks, Joyce Holland, Pat Johnson, Melanie Long, Karen Matthew, Susan McDonald, Cindi Morrison, Patricia O'Neil, Carla Rains, Joyce Robinson, Laura Rowan, Susan Sego, Amy Taylor, Trish Vines, Jane Walker, Andrea Westbrook, and Sally White.

STITCHING TIP

Working over Two Fabric Threads: Use the sewing method instead of the stab method when working over two fabric threads. To use the sewing method, keep your stitching hand on the right side of the fabric (instead of stabbing the fabric with the needle and taking your stitching hand to the back of the fabric to pick up the needle). With the sewing method, you take the needle down and up with one stroke instead of two. To add support to stitches, it is important that the first Cross Stitch is placed on the fabric with stitch 1-2 beginning and ending where a vertical fabric thread crosses over a horizontal fabric thread (**Fig. 4**). When the first stitch is in the correct position, the entire design will be placed properly, with vertical fabric threads supporting each stitch.

Fig. 4

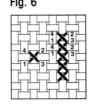

STITCH DIAGRAMS

Note: Bring threaded needle up at 1 and all odd numbers and down at 2 and all even numbers.

Counted Cross Stitch (X): Work one Cross Stitch to correspond to each colored square on the chart. For horizontal rows, work stitches in two journeys (**Fig. 5**). For vertical rows, complete each stitch as shown (**Fig. 6**). When working over two fabric threads, work Cross Stitch as shown in **Fig. 7**. When the chart shows a Backstitch crossing a colored square (**Fig. 8**), a Cross Stitch should be worked first; then the Backstitch (**Fig. 13** or **14**) should be worked on top of the Cross Stitch.

Fig. 5   **Fig. 6**

Fig. 7   **Fig. 8**

Quarter Stitch (¼X and ¾X): Quarter Stitches are denoted by triangular shapes of color on the chart and on the color key. For a One-Quarter Stitch, come up at 1 (**Fig. 9**), then split fabric thread to go down at 2. When stitches 1-4 are worked in the same color, the resulting stitch is called a Three-Quarter Stitch (**¾X**). **Fig. 10** shows the technique for Quarter Stitches when working over two fabric threads.

Fig. 9   **Fig. 10**

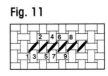
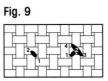

Half Cross Stitch (½X): This stitch is one journey of the Cross Stitch and is worked from lower left to upper right as shown in **Fig. 11**. When working over two fabric threads, work Half Cross Stitch as shown in **Fig. 12**.

Fig. 11   **Fig. 12**

Backstitch (B'ST): For outline detail, Backstitch (shown on chart and on color key by black or colored straight lines) should be worked after the design has been completed (**Fig. 13**). When working over two fabric threads, work Backstitch as shown in **Fig. 14**.

Fig. 13   **Fig. 14**

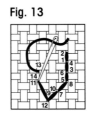
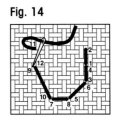

French Knot: Bring needle up at 1. Wrap floss once around needle and insert needle at 2, holding end of floss with non-stitching fingers (**Fig. 15**). Tighten knot, then pull needle through fabric, holding floss until it must be released. For larger knot, use more strands of floss; wrap only once.

Fig. 15

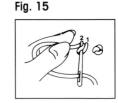

Continued on page 96.

FINISHING INSTRUCTIONS

The Night Before Christmas Stockings (shown on page 11, charts on page 57): For each stocking, you will need a 10" x 17" piece of fabric for cuff backing, two 13" x 20" pieces of fabric for stocking, two 13" x 20" pieces of fabric for stocking lining, 23" length of $1/4$" dia. purchased cording with attached seam allowance, tracing paper, and fabric marking pencil.

For cuff pattern, fold tracing paper in half and place fold on dashed line of Cuff Pattern; trace pattern onto tracing paper. Add a $1/2$" seam allowance on all sides and cut out pattern. Unfold and press flat.

Centering design horizontally with top of design $2^{1}/4$" from top of pattern, pin pattern in place. Use fabric marking pencil to draw around pattern; remove pattern and cut out on drawn line. Use Cuff Pattern to cut out cuff backing fabric.

Matching right sides and short edges, fold cuff in half. Using a $1/2$" seam allowance, sew short edges together. Repeat for cuff backing.

If needed, trim seam allowance of cording to $1/2$". Matching raw edges and beginning at back seam, pin cording to lower edge of right side of stitched piece. Ends of cording should overlap approximately 4". Turn overlapped ends of cording toward outside edge of stitched piece; baste cording to stitched piece.

Matching right sides and raw edges, use a $1/2$" seam allowance to sew stitched piece and cuff backing fabric together along lower edge. Trim seam allowance at point and clip curves. Turn cuff right side out and press; baste raw edges together.

For stocking pattern, match arrows of Stocking Pattern to form one pattern and trace pattern onto tracing paper; add a $1/2$" seam allowance on all sides and cut out pattern. Matching right sides and raw edges, place stocking fabric pieces together; place pattern on fabric pieces and pin pattern in place. Use fabric marking pencil to draw around pattern; remove pattern and cut out on drawn line. Repeat with lining fabric pieces.

Matching right sides and leaving top open, use a $1/2$" seam allowance to sew stocking pieces together. Clip seam allowance at curves and turn stocking right side out.

Matching right sides and leaving top open, use a $5/8$" seam allowance to sew lining pieces together; trim seam allowance close to stitching. **Do not turn lining right side out.** With wrong sides facing, place lining inside stocking. Baste stocking and lining together close to raw edges.

Matching raw edges, place right side of cuff to inside of stocking with cuff back seam at center back of stocking. Use a $1/2$" seam allowance to sew cuff and stocking together. Fold cuff $6^{1}/2$" to outside of stocking and press.

STOCKING
BOTTOM

STOCKING
TOP

CUFF